RIOU

Suez Remastered

GARY LEE KVAMME

Volume 2

Telling Art Series

RIOU

Suez Remastered

I

Édouard Riou was born in 1833 in Saint-Servan, Ille-et-Vilaine and died in Paris in 1900. He was a Pre-Impressionist painter, a renowned illustrator of books by Jules Verne and Alexandre Dumas, and a contributor to the weekly newspaper *Le tour du monde*, and in 1870, at the request of Ferdinand de Lesseps, he created a series of watercolors to commemorate the inauguration of the Suez Canal in November 1869. One of the paintings (page 30) is a sort of oriental reverie; three grandstands built for the guests of honor at the religious ceremony for the inauguration of the canal on 16 November stand set against a beautiful sky. In the foreground, Egyptians gather for the ceremony. In the background, emerging almost out of nowhere, prows of ships ready to sail down the canal prefigure the revolution in economic and diplomatic relations brought about by the Suez Canal. On the following day, 17 November, the imperial yacht *L'Aigle* led the procession and entered the channel.

The magnificent inaugural ceremonies lasted three weeks. Many notable political and literary figures attended the celebration, among them the Austrian emperor Franz Joseph, the king of Hungary, the prince of Prussia, and the prince and princess of Holland. Undoubtedly the most valued guest, was the French empress Eugénie, for whom the khedive built a palace on the Nile, a replica of her private apartments in the Tuileries.

Among the scholars and writers were the famous German Egyptologist Richard Lepsius, The Norwegian playwright Henrik Ibsen, the French painter Jean-Léon Gérôme,

1

and the French writer Théophile Gautier. A large contingent of journalists was also present.

The vast human and technical enterprise of the digging of the Suez Canal (1859-1869), which linked the Red and the Mediterranean Seas, was the work of the diplomat Ferdinand de Lesseps (1805-1894). De Lesseps knew Egypt well; indeed he had held various diplomatic posts from 1828 to 1837 and was commissioned by the viceroy Mehmet Ali to "finish" the education of the latter's son, Saïd. And since he was a cousin of the Empress Eugénie's mother, de Lesseps also had privileged access to the imperial couple. When his former pupil, the viceroy Saïd, came to power in 1854, de Lesseps seized the opportunity to revive his project of digging a canal through the Suez isthmus. An Egyptian governmental measure or firman dated 30 November, 1854, granted him permission not only to set up a company for the digging of the channel but also to exploit the canal for 99 years after commissioning, though necessarily pending the final approval of the Turkish sultan, the Egyptian viceroy sovereign. A second text, signed 5 January, 1856, defined the channel as a neutral waterway, and opened it to all merchant vessels without distinction of nationality, in return for payment of a transit fee. In December 1858, the Suez Canal Universal Company was finally constituted, and in Europe shares in the project were snapped up. In England, however, the government feared the development of the French influence in Egypt that could have harmed British interests in India, and was far from supporting the project; indeed it launched a campaign against Lesseps.

Nevertheless, the ceremonial first blow of the pickaxe inaugurating work on the channel was struck near Pelusium on Easter Monday, 25 April, 1859. Ishmael, successor of Saïd who died in 1863, challenged the previous agreements with de Lesseps, but the mediation of Napoleon III relieved tensions. The agreement of 6 July, 1864, granted compensation of 84 million gold francs and ceded 10,864 hectares to the Canal Company; the freshwater canal built to feed the construction site was handed to Egypt. On 19 March, 1866, a firman of Sultan Abd-ul-Aziz ratified this agreement.

Once diplomatic tensions were eased, work could continue. On 15 August, 1869, the waters of the Mediterranean finally mingled with those of the Red Sea in the Bitter Lakes. The maritime canal was 164 km long, from Suez to Port Saïd, located just west of Pelusium, 54 meters wide, 8 meters deep. Three cities were founded (Suez, Ismailia, Port Saïd) and two ports equipped (Suez and Port Saïd).

While the opening of the channel by the Empress Eugénie cemented Franco-Egyptian relations, Napoleon III also needed to tread carefully in his relationship with the Sublime Porte, since the latter had become increasingly annoyed with the viceroy of Egypt's desires for autonomy, of which the Suez Canal in the end would become the symbol. Tensions were in fact only put to one side for the period of the opening ceremonies. The Empress Eugénie was first received at Constantinople by Sultan Abd-ul-Aziz. She then headed for Alexandria, landing 22 October, 1869. About three weeks later (16 November) she reached the new town of Port Saïd, which hosted the first religious ceremonies for the inauguration. The next day, to the thundering sound of a canon salute, the imperial yacht *L'Aigle* undertook the first voyage down the canal, followed by an impressive flotilla of forty ships bearing the Viceroy, the Emperor of Austria, the Crown Prince of Prussia, the princes of the Netherlands and Hanover, and the ambassadors of England and Russia. In the evening, the *L'Aigle* dropped anchor off the other new town, Ismailia, in the Temsah Lake.

Utilizing the Kvamme process of digital enhancement, the tired, timeworn Suez Canal artworks by Édouard Riou are, in the present undertaking, painstakingly restored and re-energized with a vivid and palpable sense of their original freshness and immediacy.

II

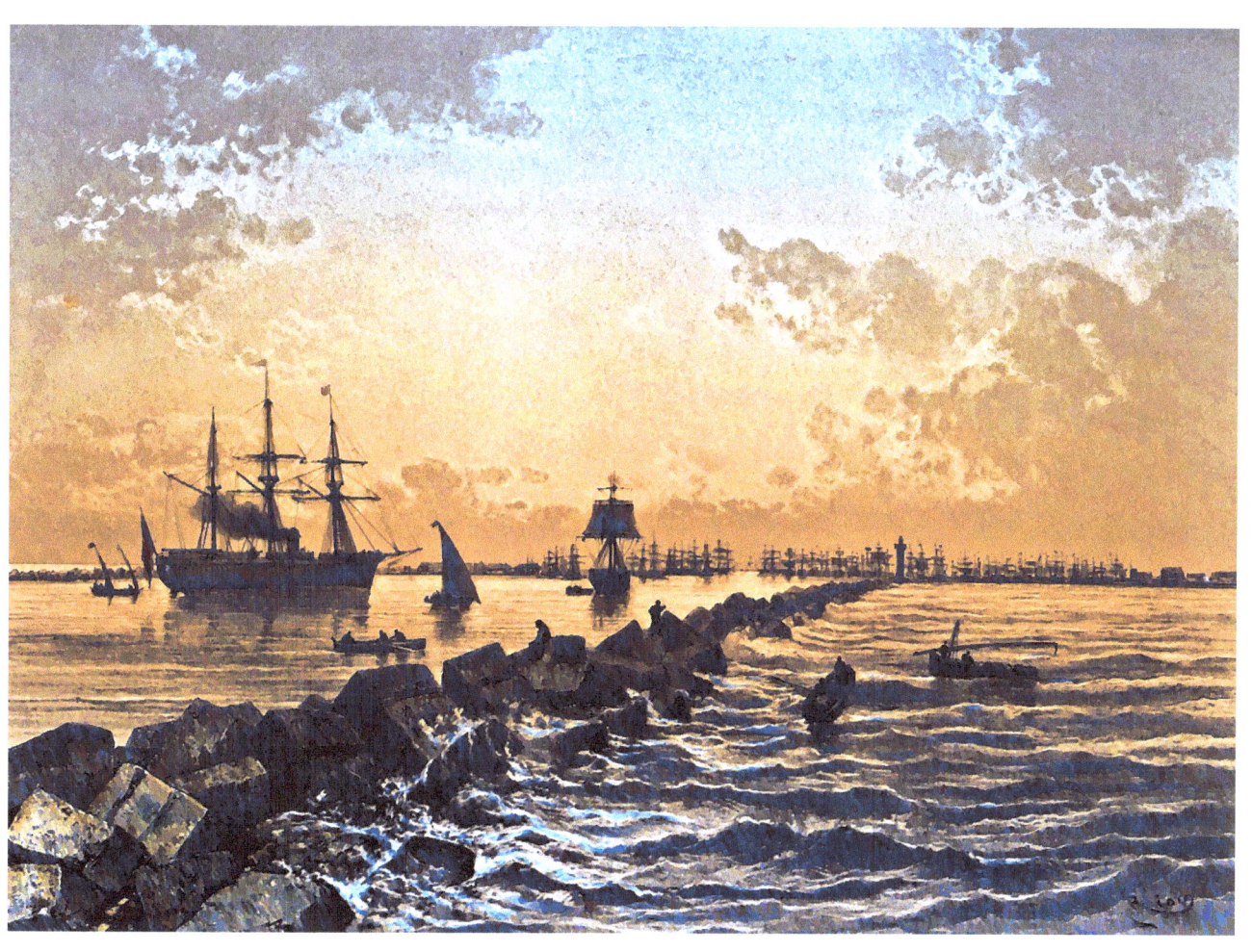

ENTRÉE DE PORT-SAÏD

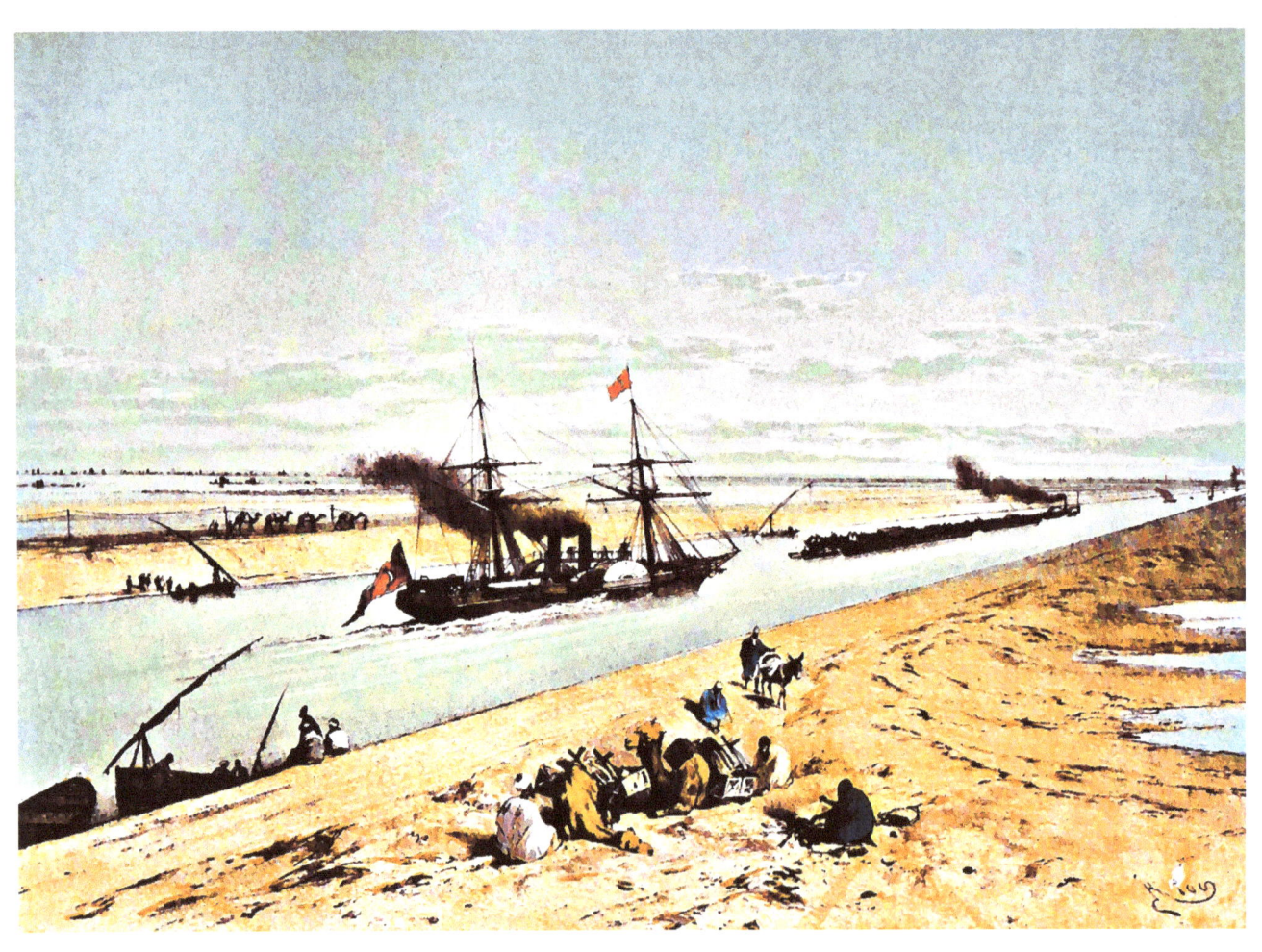

LE CANAL MARITIME A TRAVERS LE LAC MENZALEH

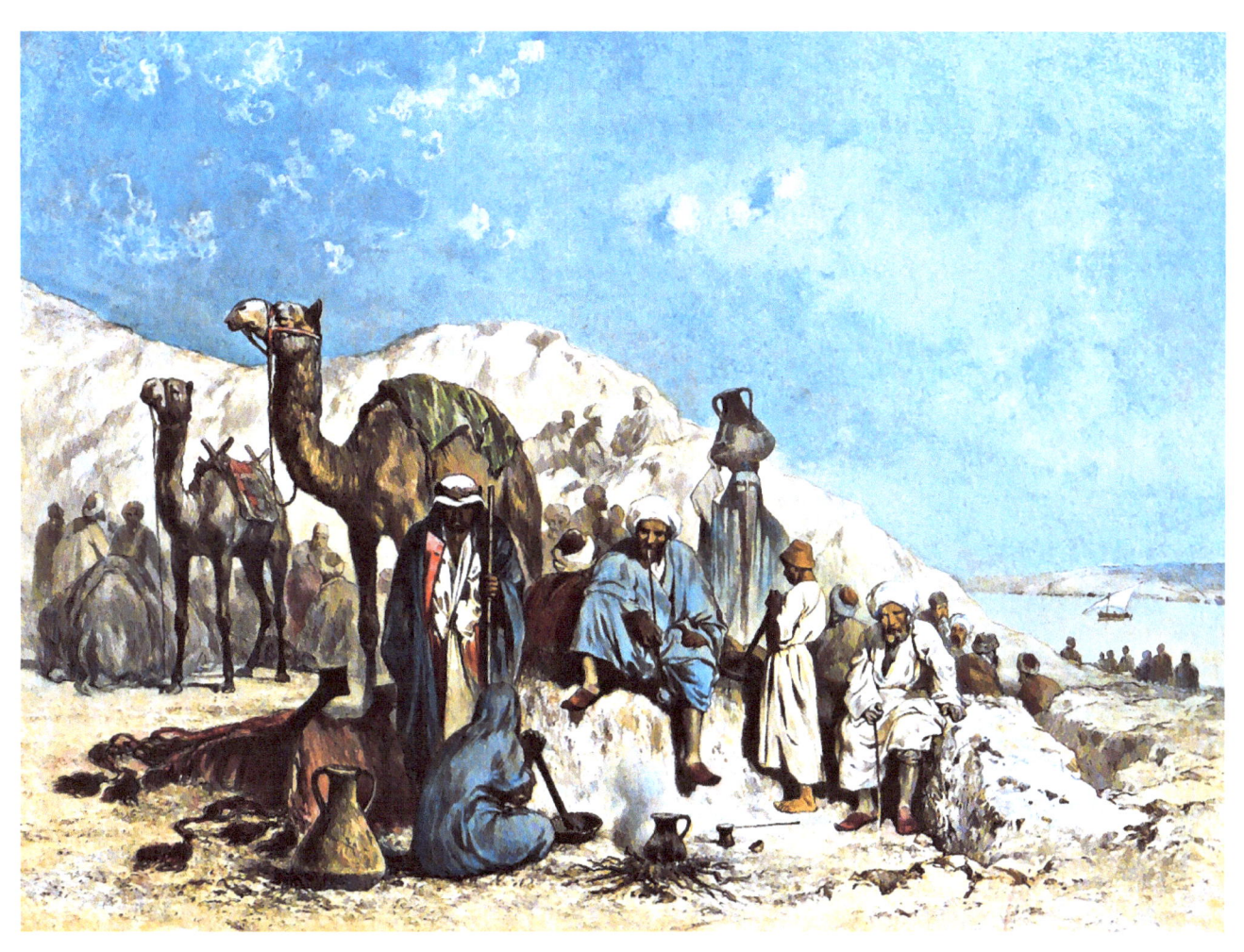

CARAVANES ATTENDANT LE BAC A KANTARA

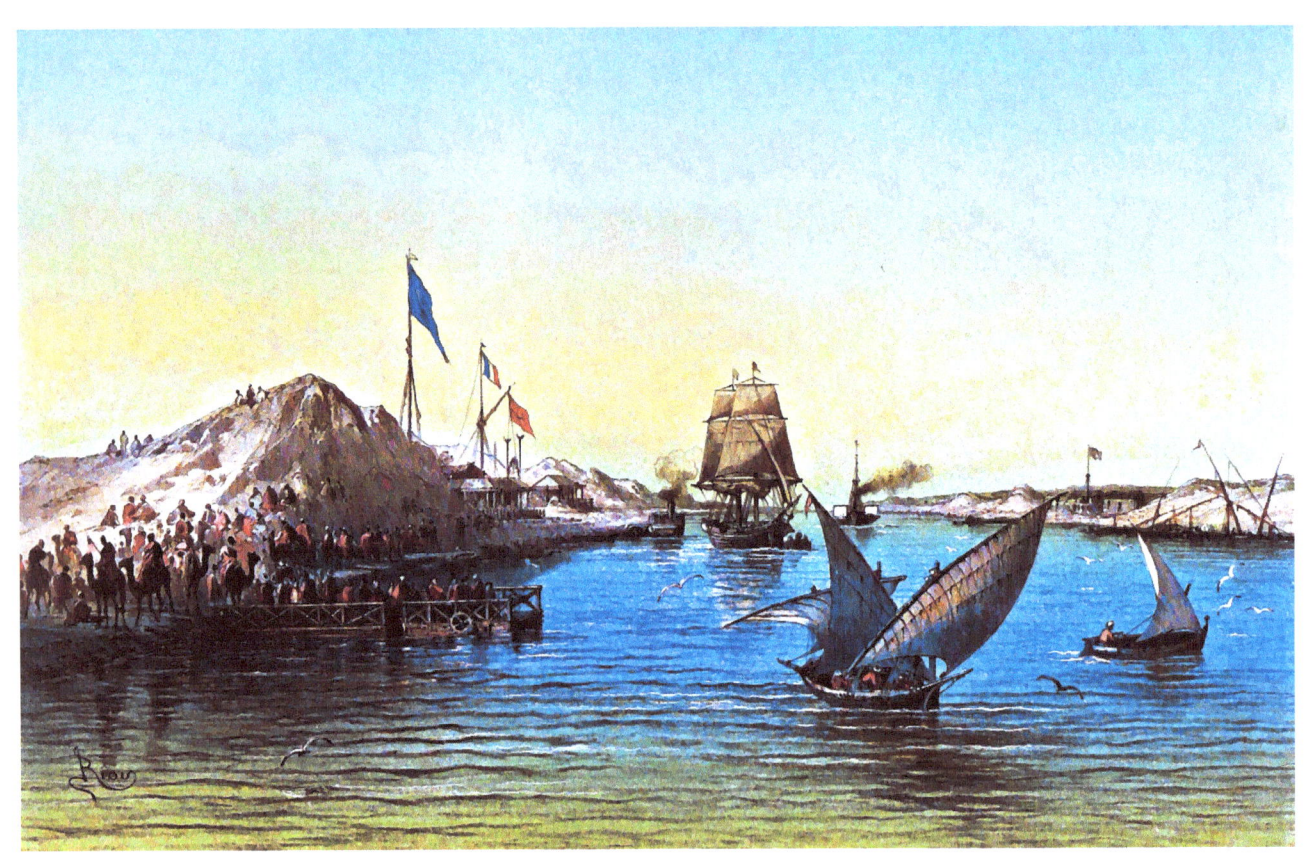

VUE DE KANTARA

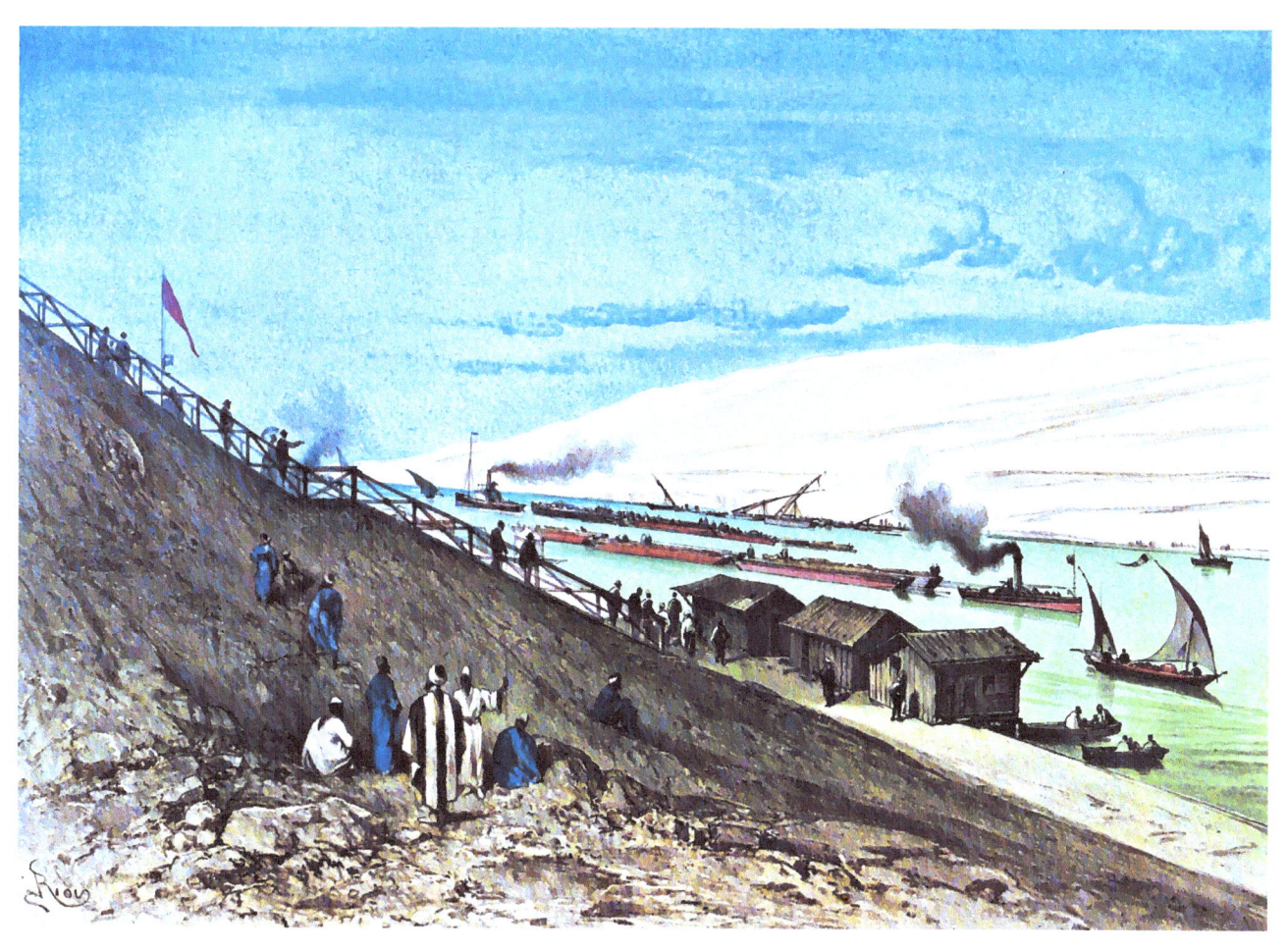

LE SEUIL D'EL-GUISR, PRIS DE LA RIVE ASIE

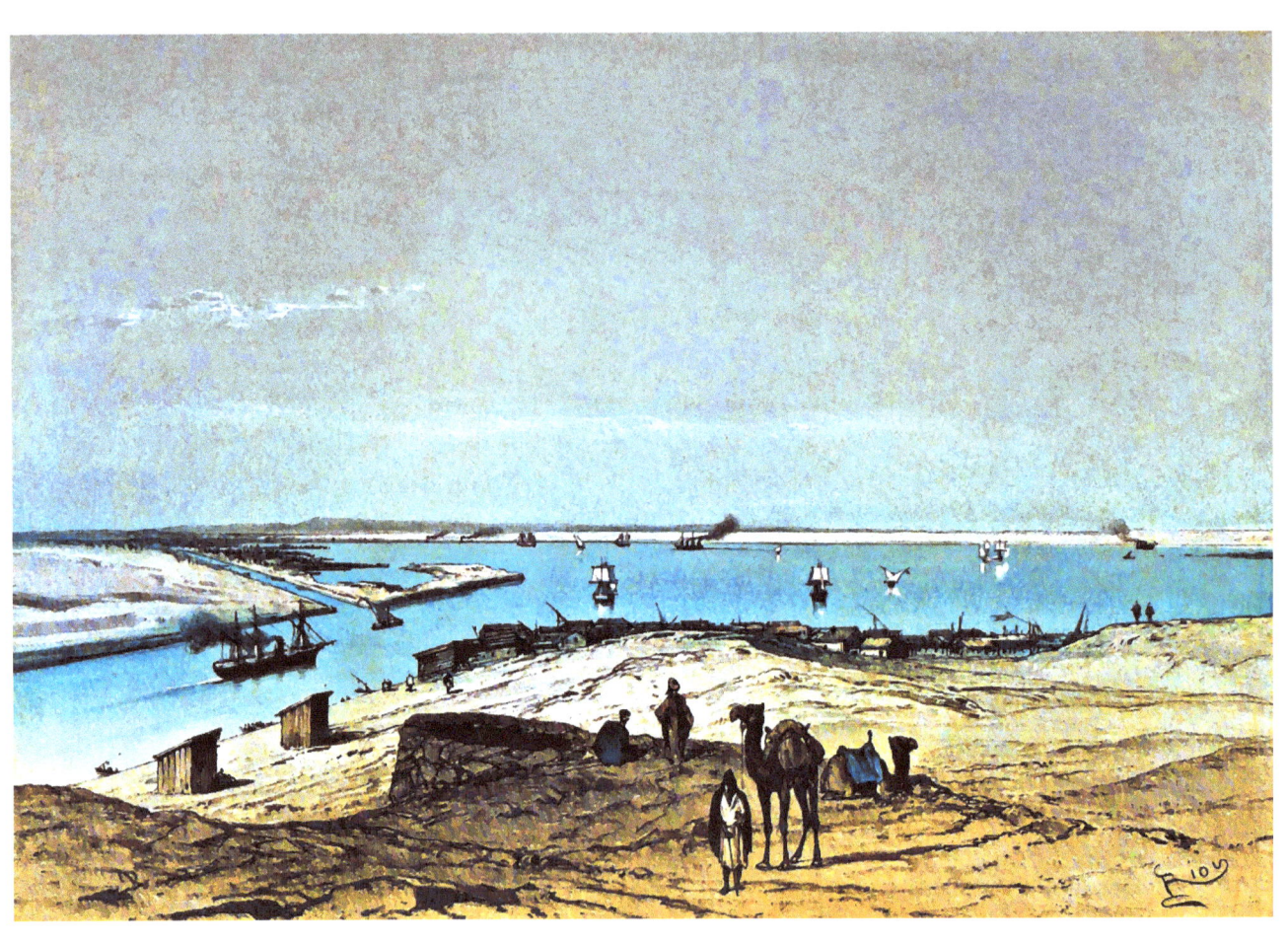

LE LAC TIMSAH, VU DU CHALET DU VICE-ROI

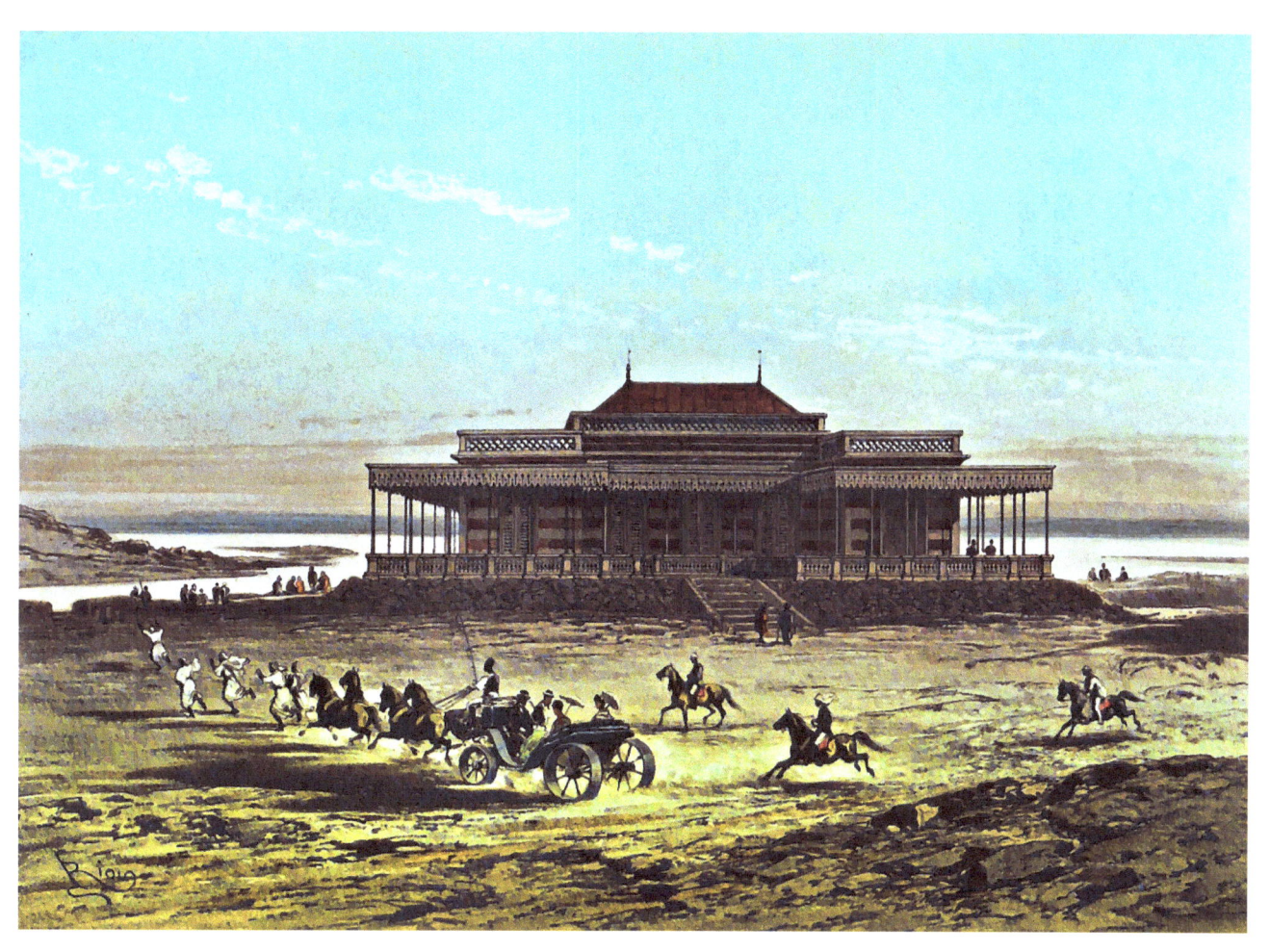

CHALET DU VICE-ROI

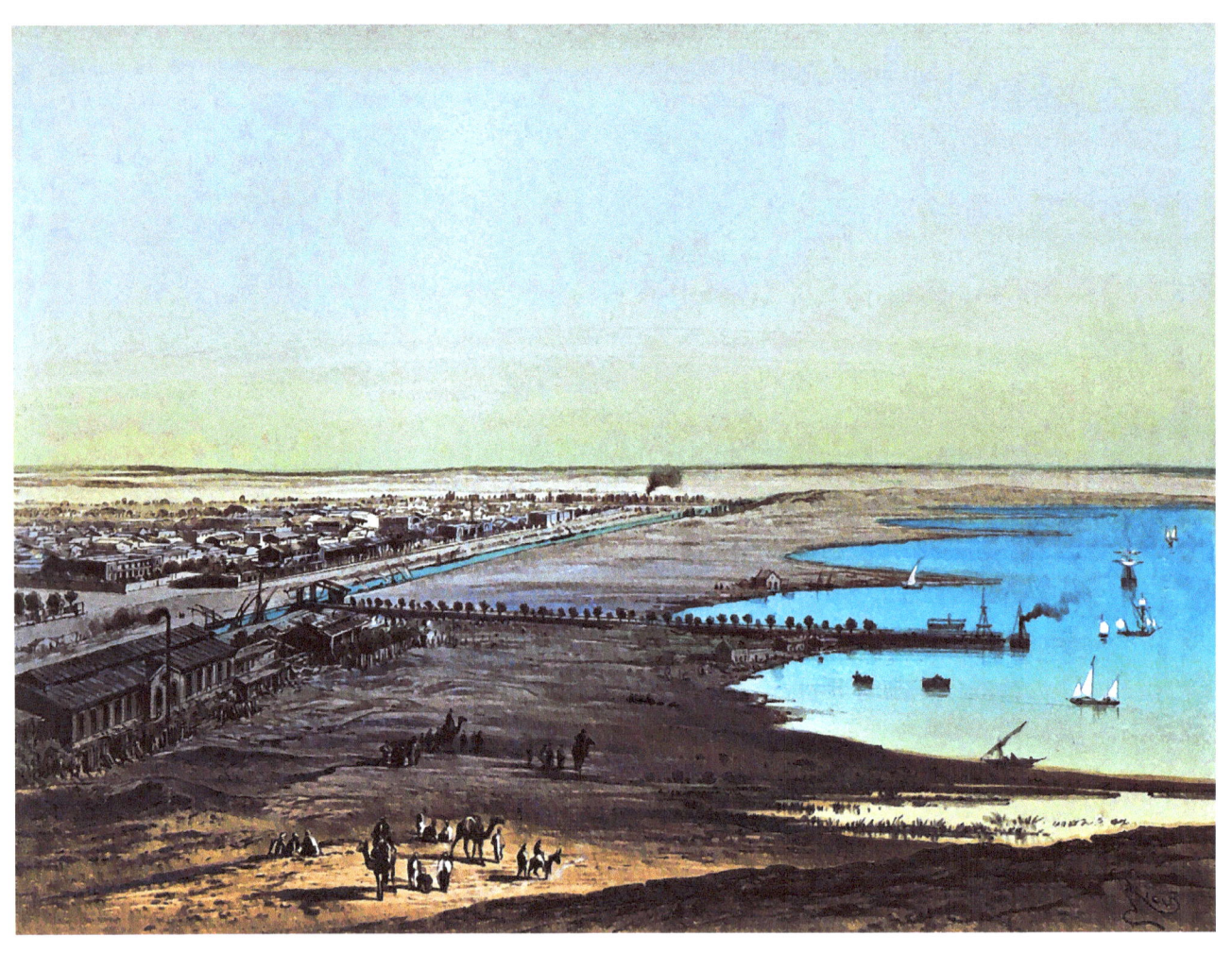

VUE D'ISMAILIA

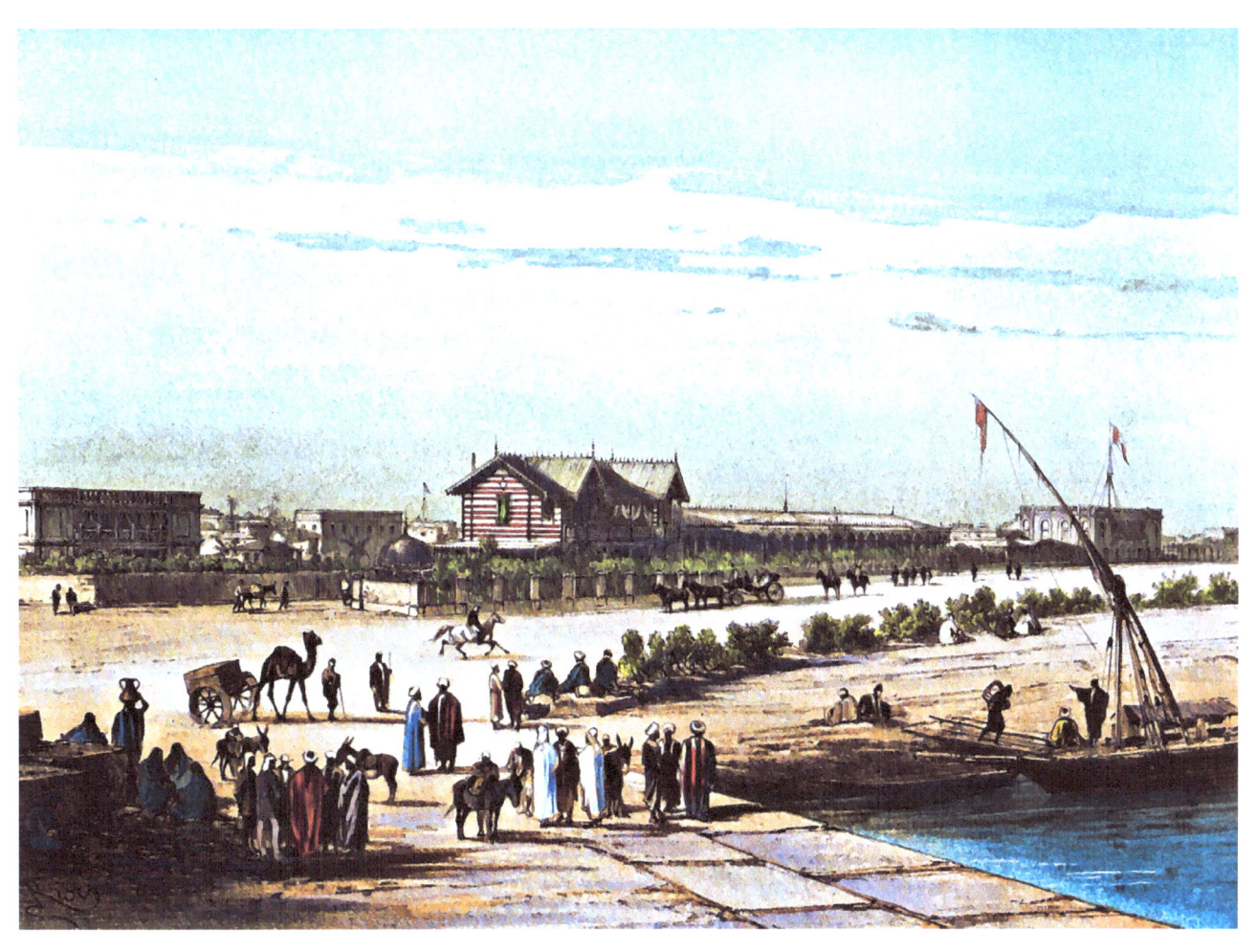

QUAI D'ISMAILIA

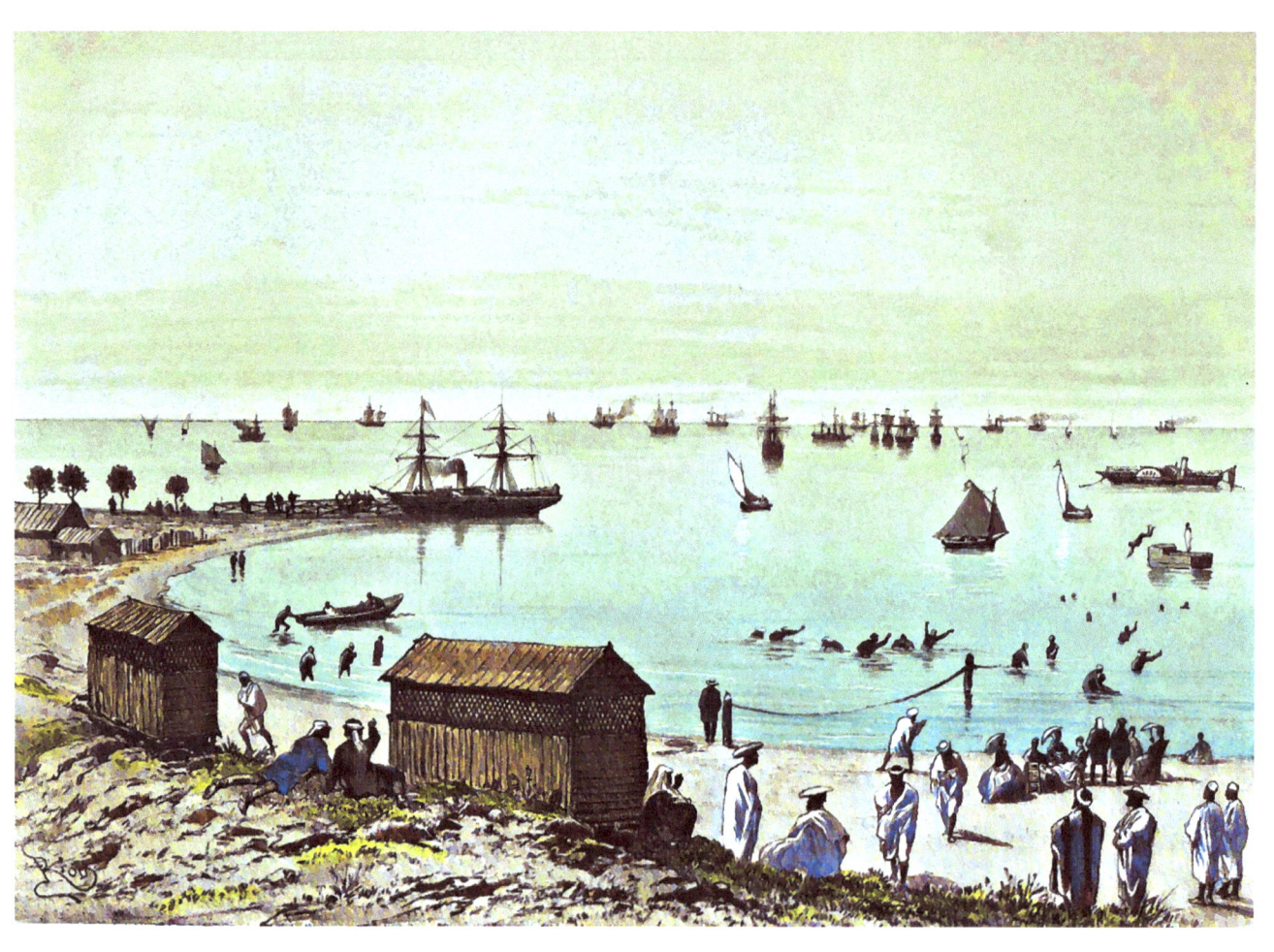

LES BAINS DE MER ET LA FLOTTILLE SUR LE LAC TIMSAH (ISMAILIA)

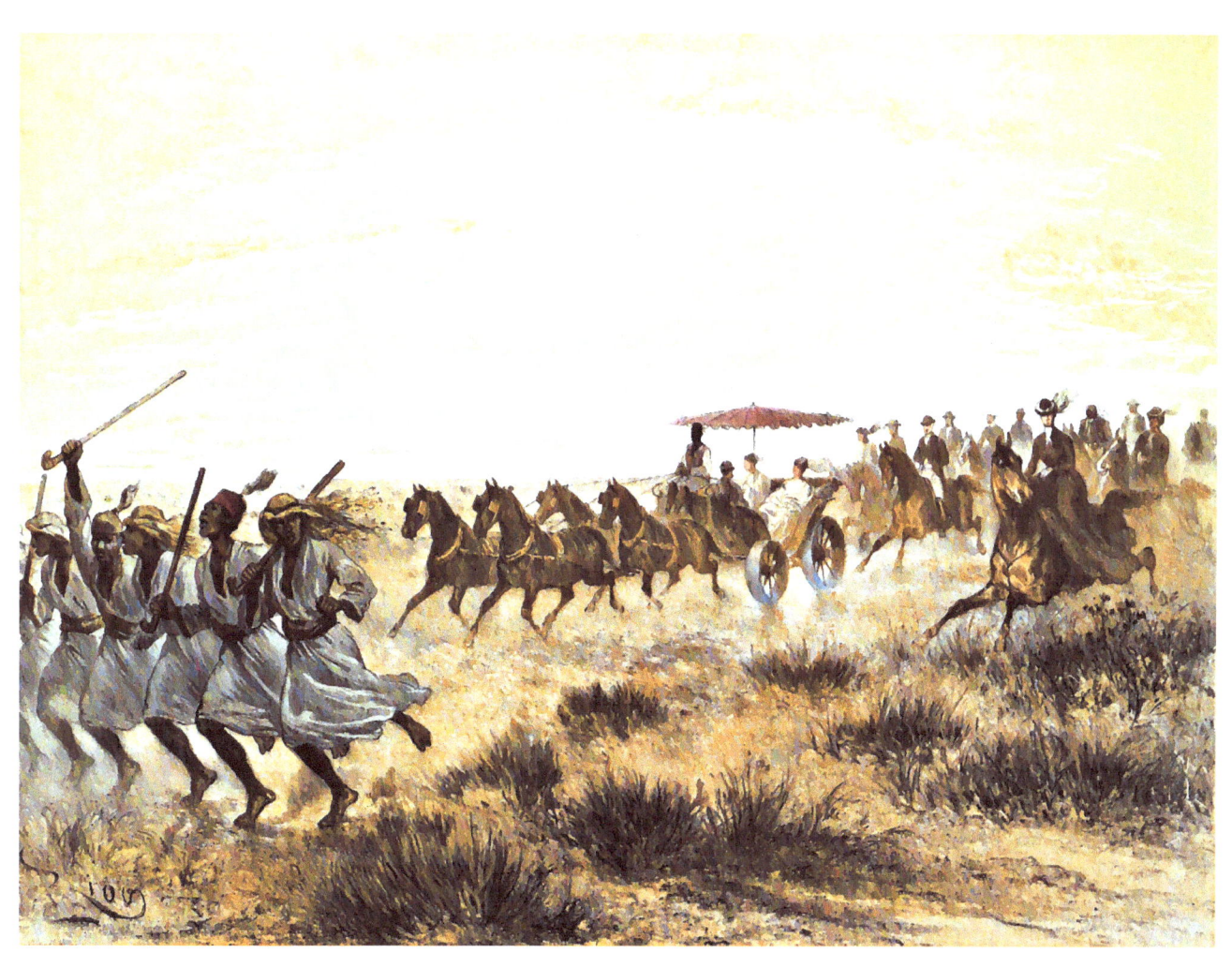

CAVALCADE AU DÉSERT

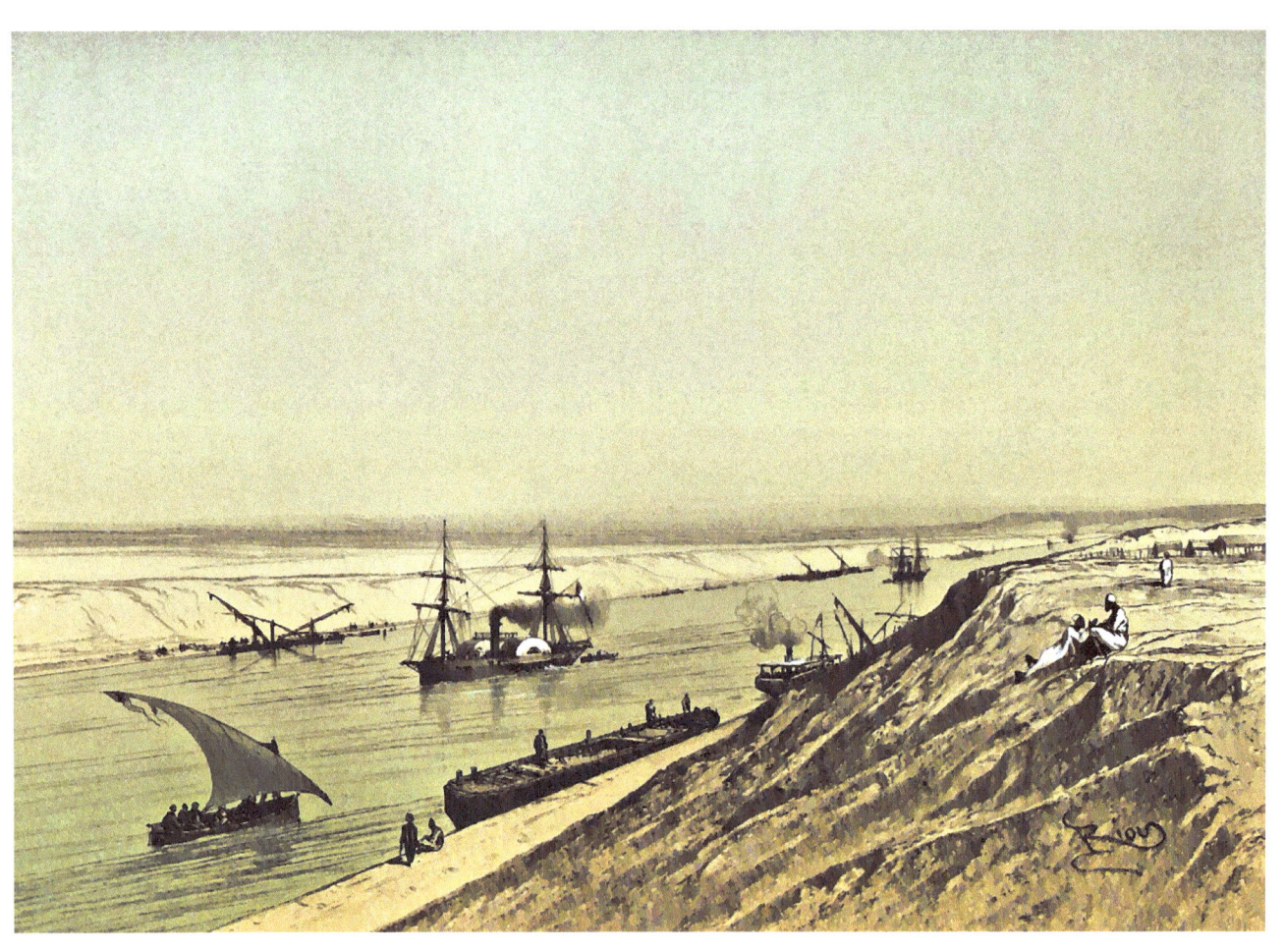

LE CANAL MARITIME AU SERAPEUM

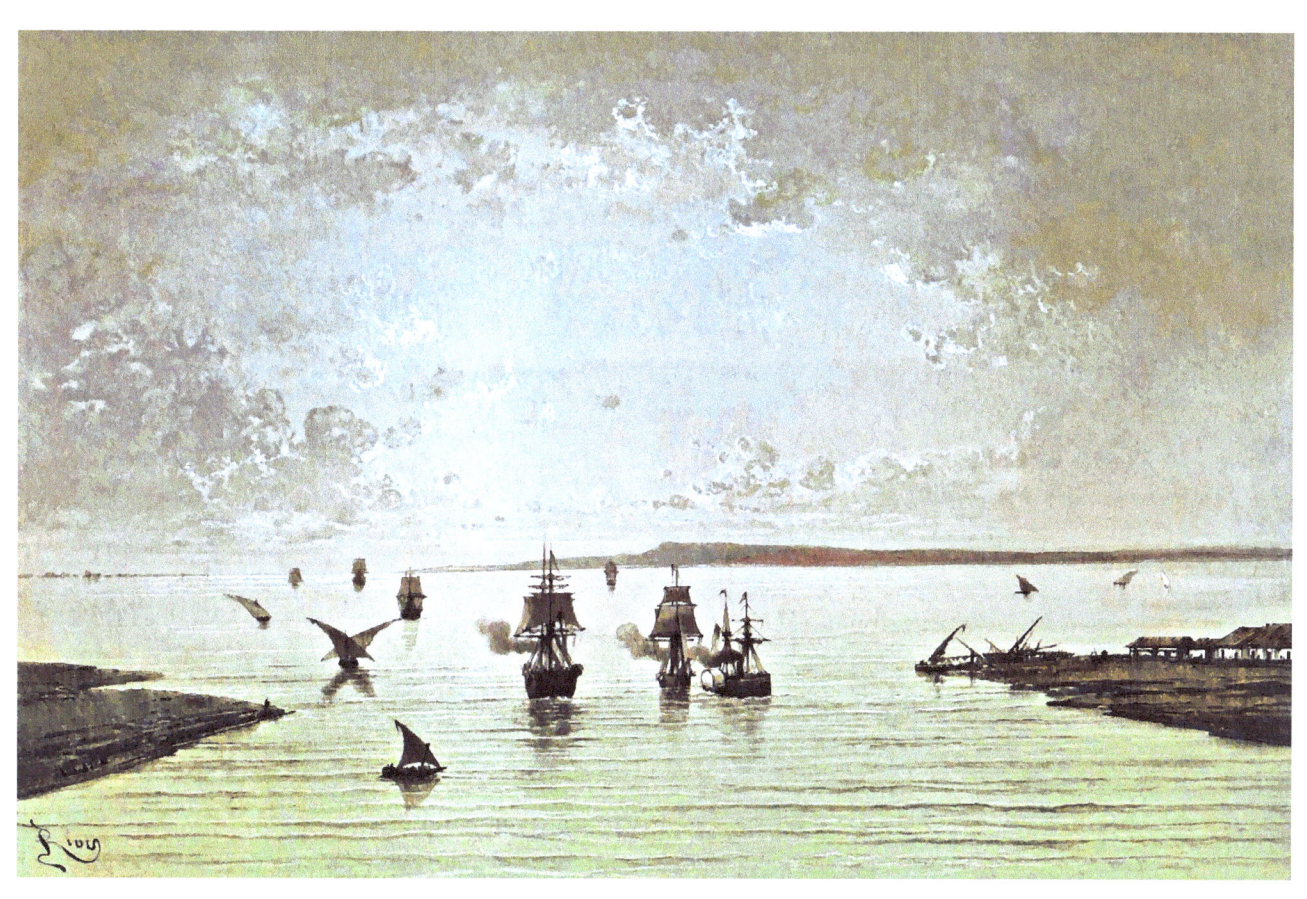

ENTRÉE DES LACS AMERS

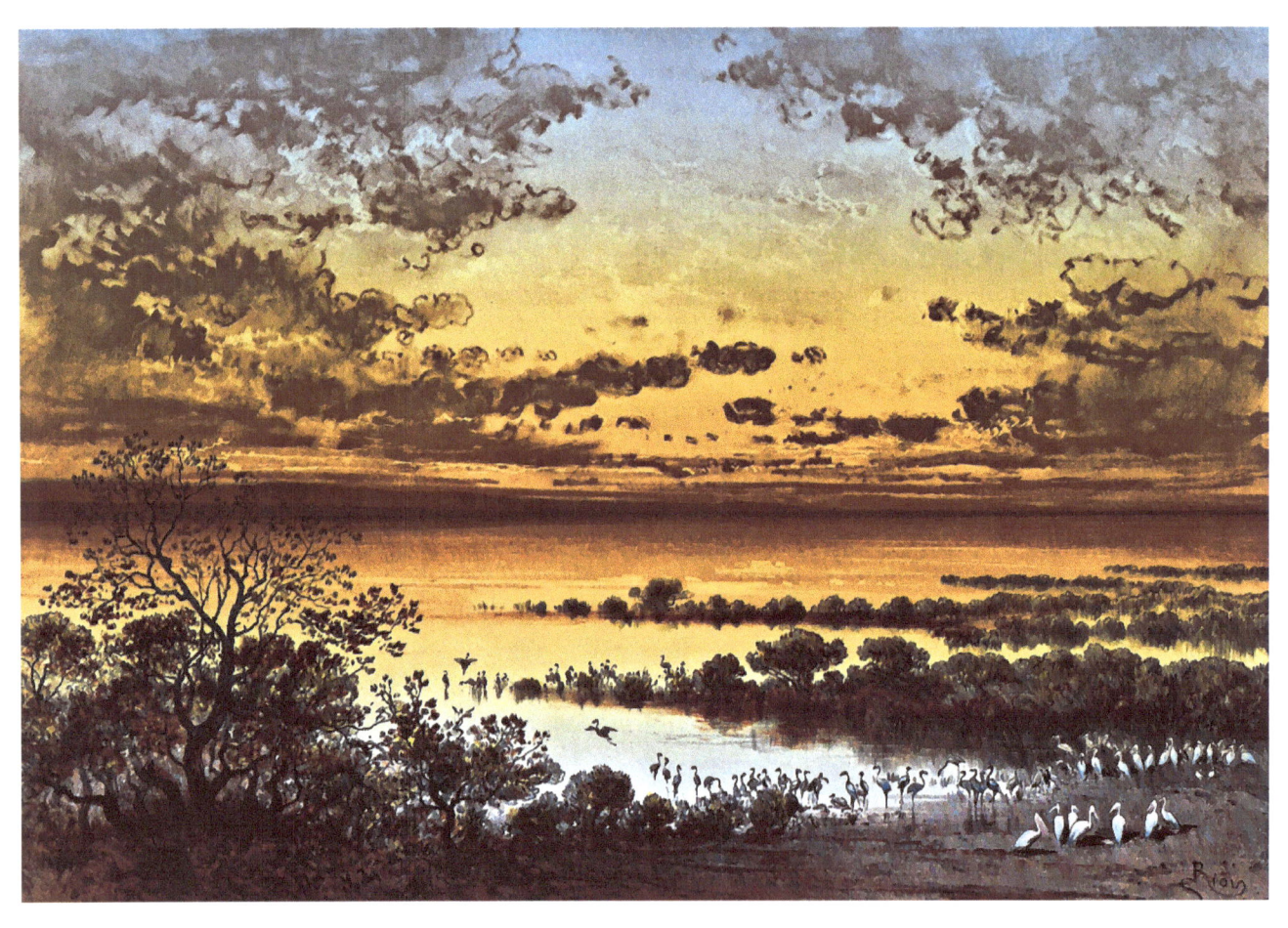

FORÊT NOYÉE D'EL-AMBAK (LACS AMERS)

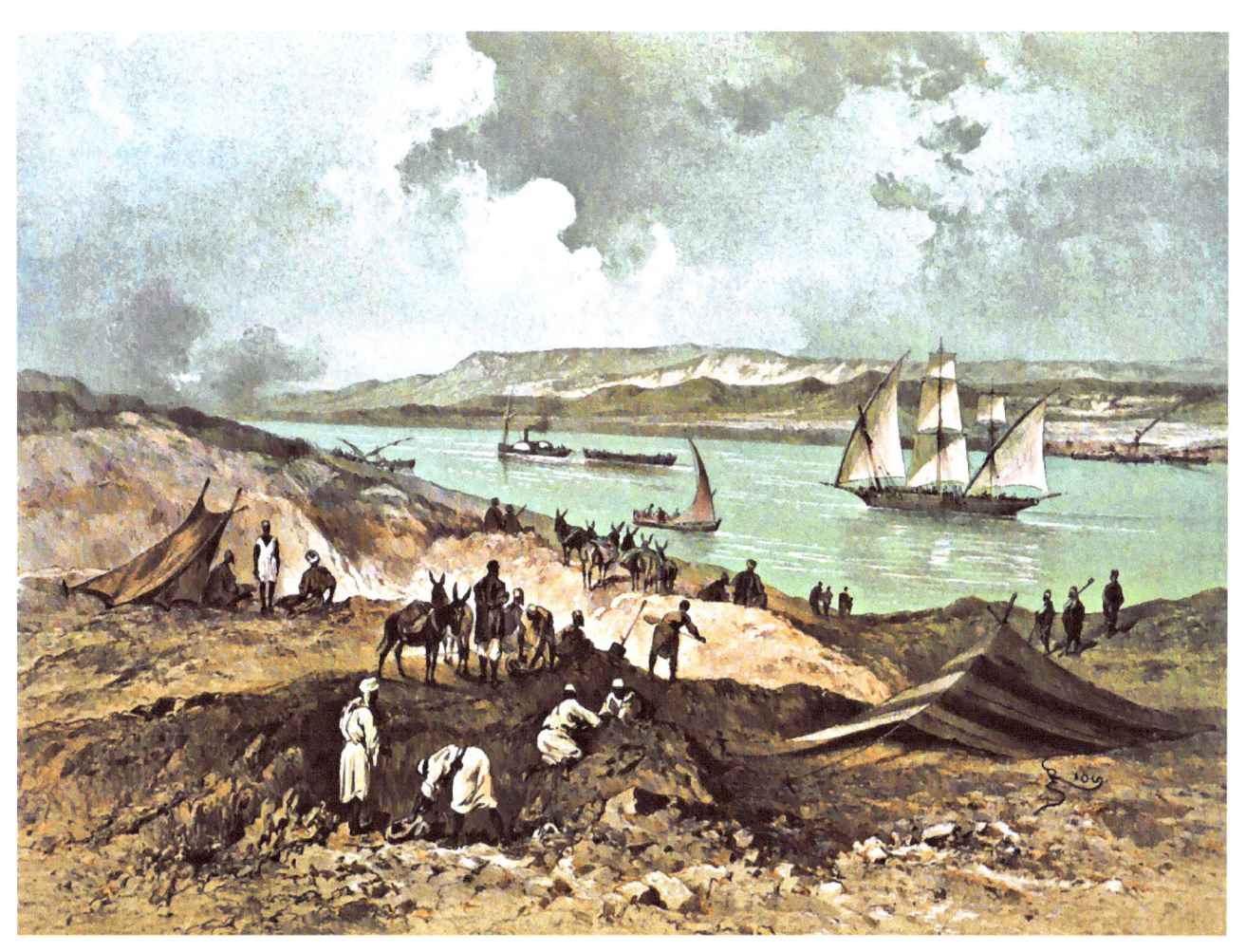

CHALOUF

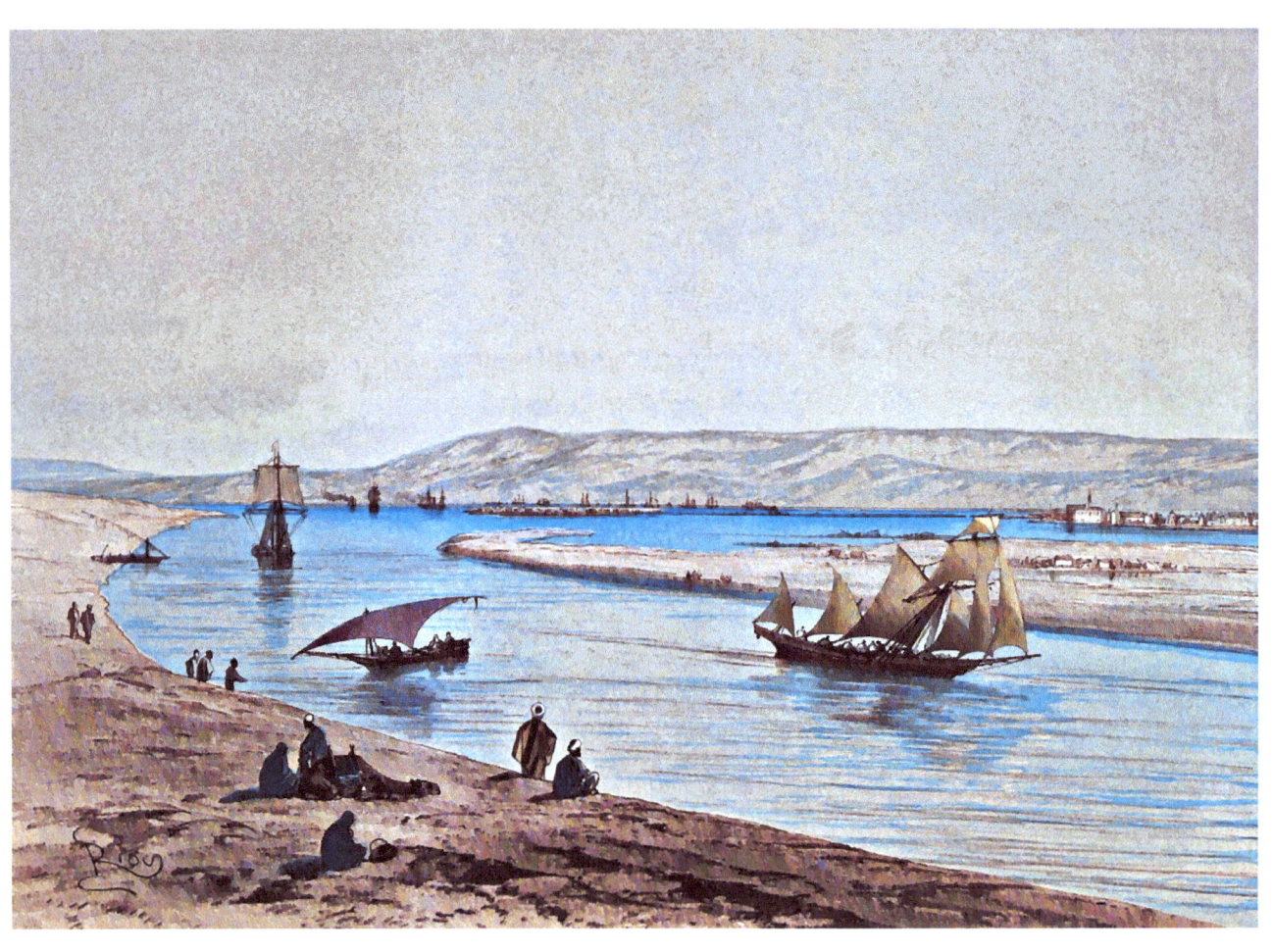

SUEZ, VUE PRISE DU CANAL MARITIME

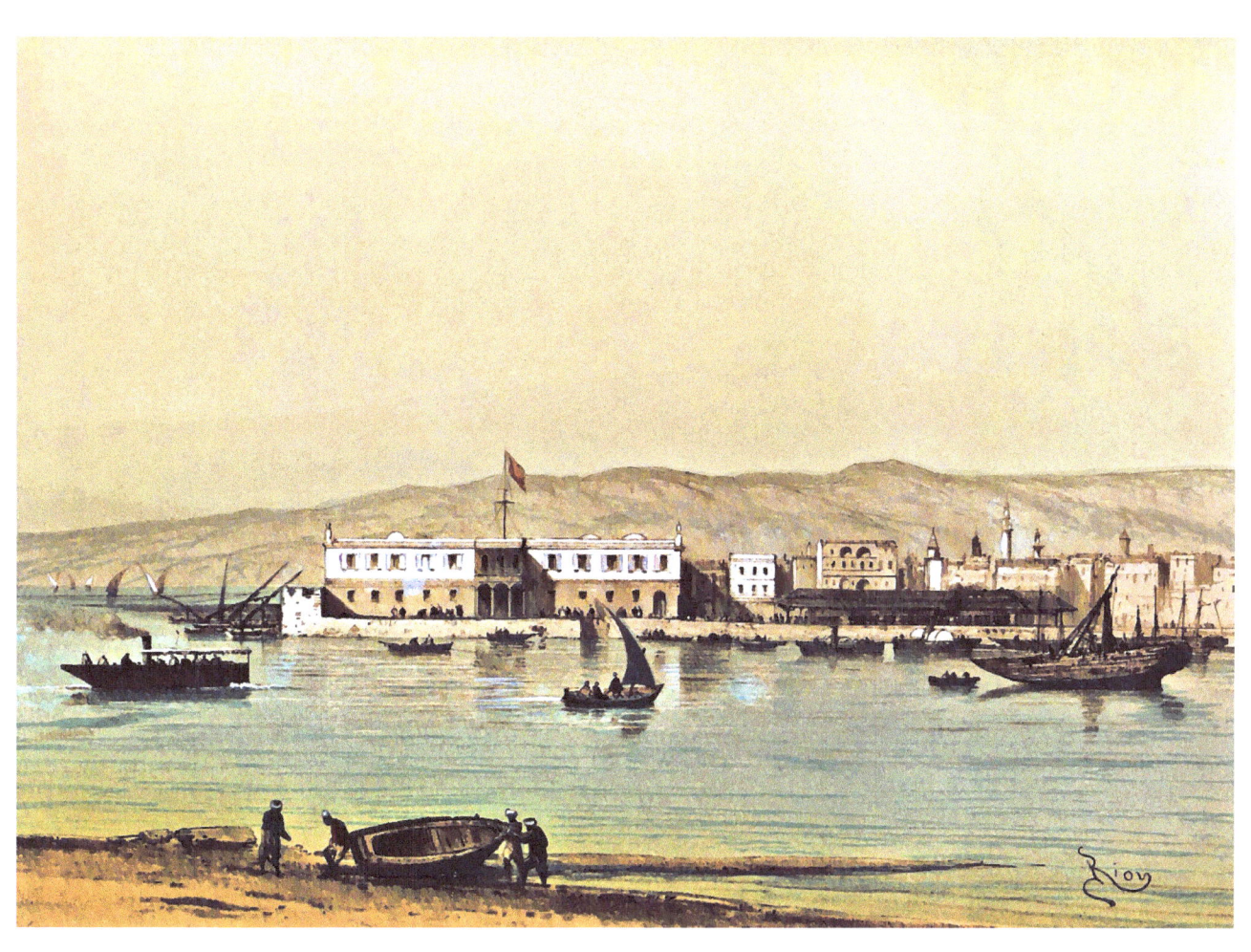

LE QUAI DE SUEZ; ARRIVÉE DE LA MALLE DES INDES

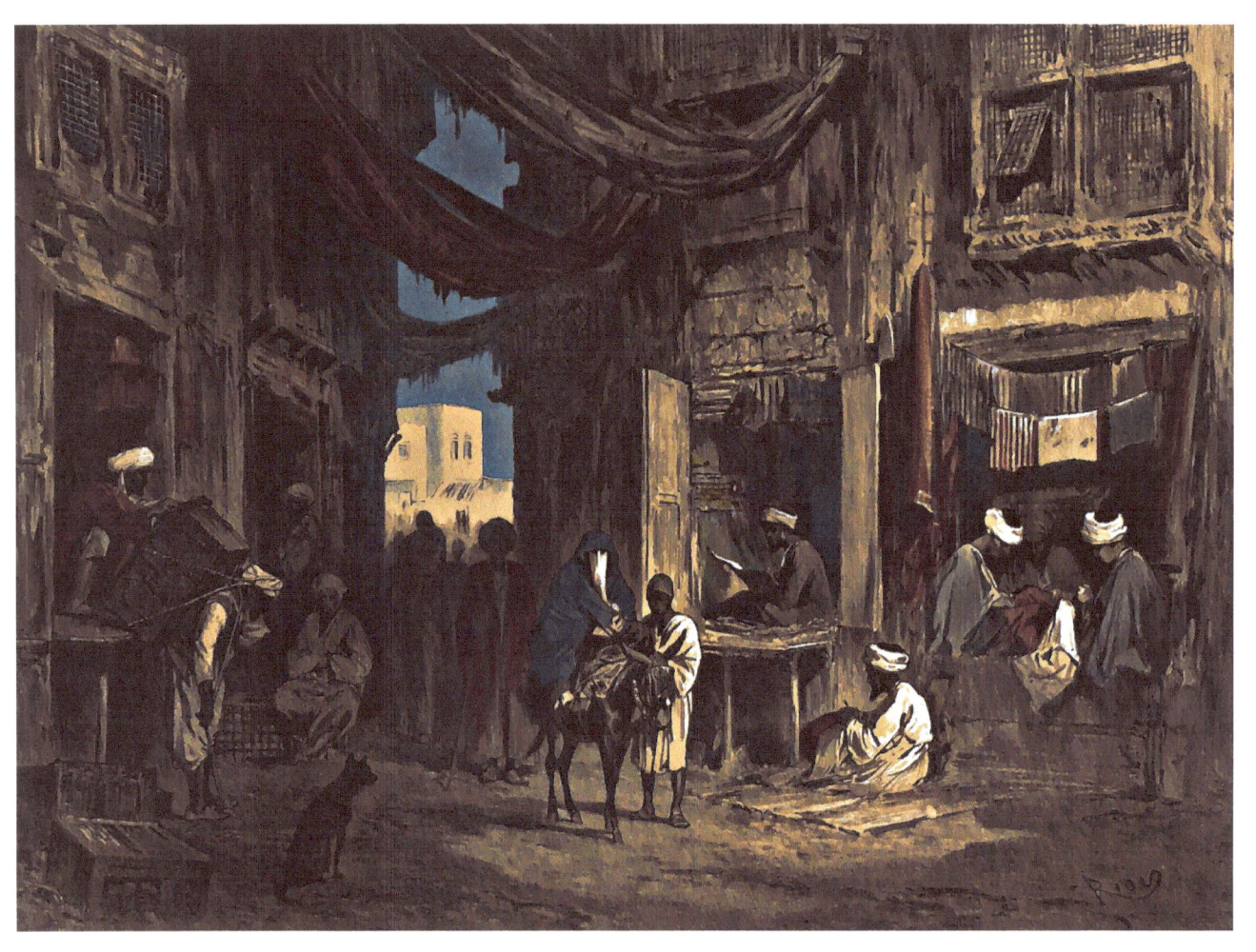

UNE RUE AU BAZAR DE SUEZ

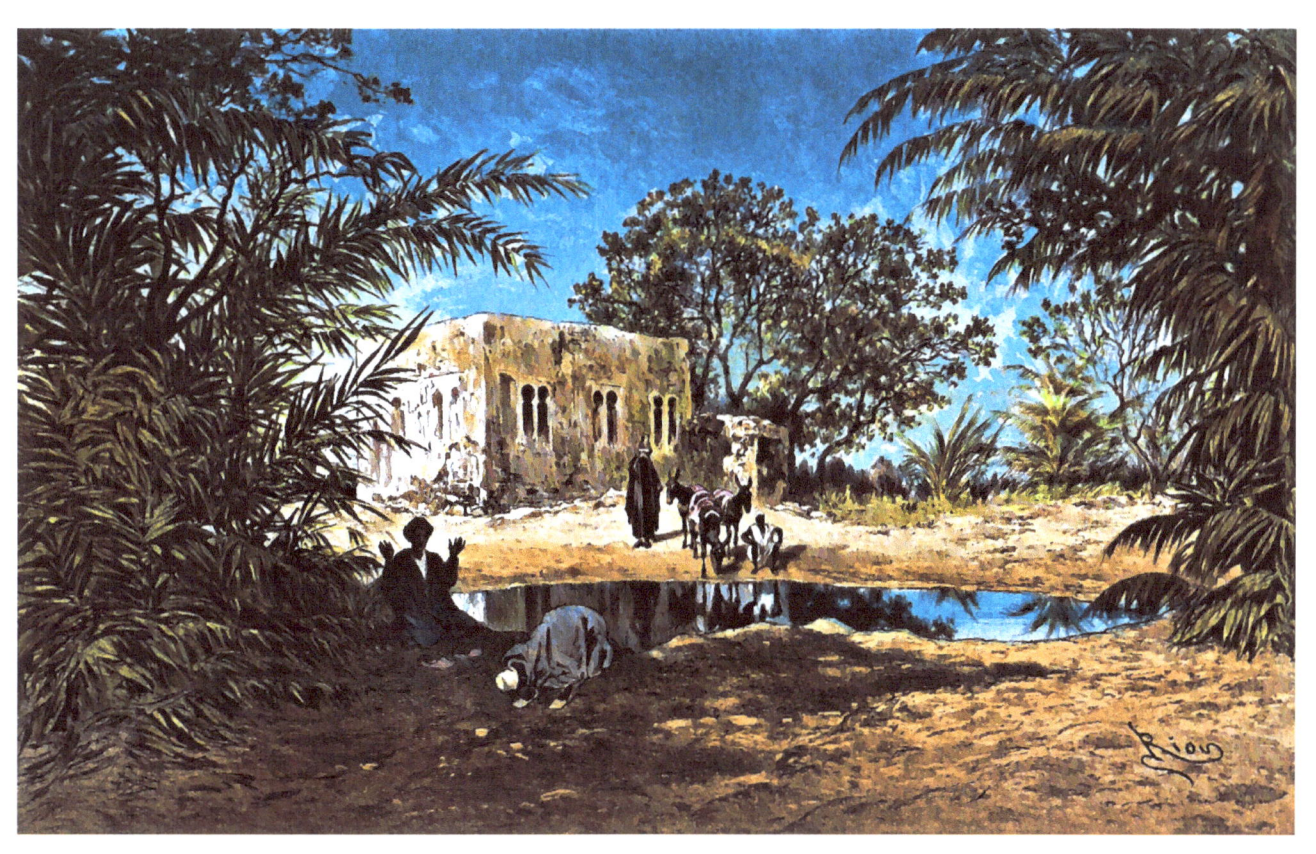

FONTAINES DE MOÏSE

III

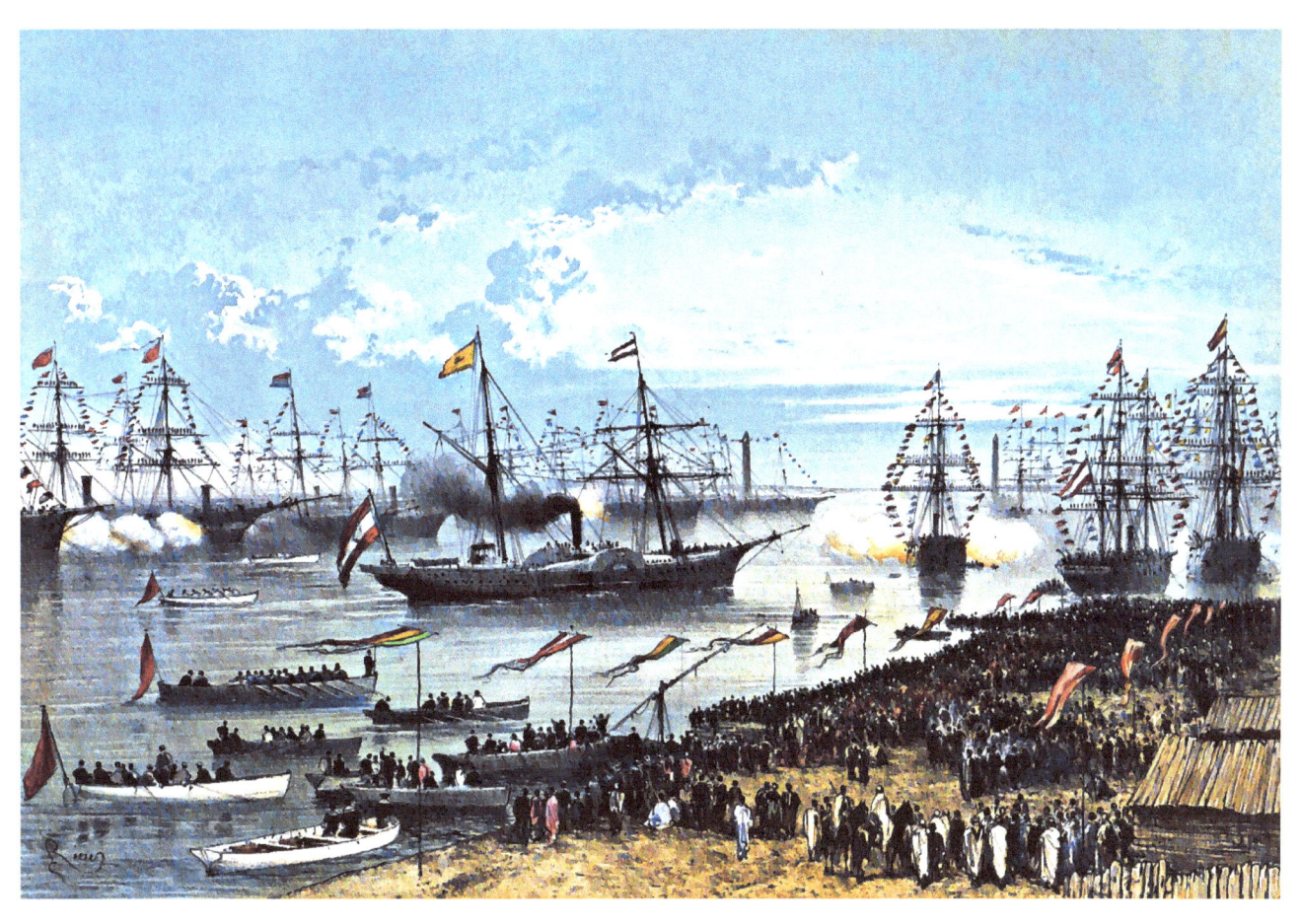

ARRIVÉE DE S.M. L'EMPEREUR D'AUTRICHE A PORT-SAÏD

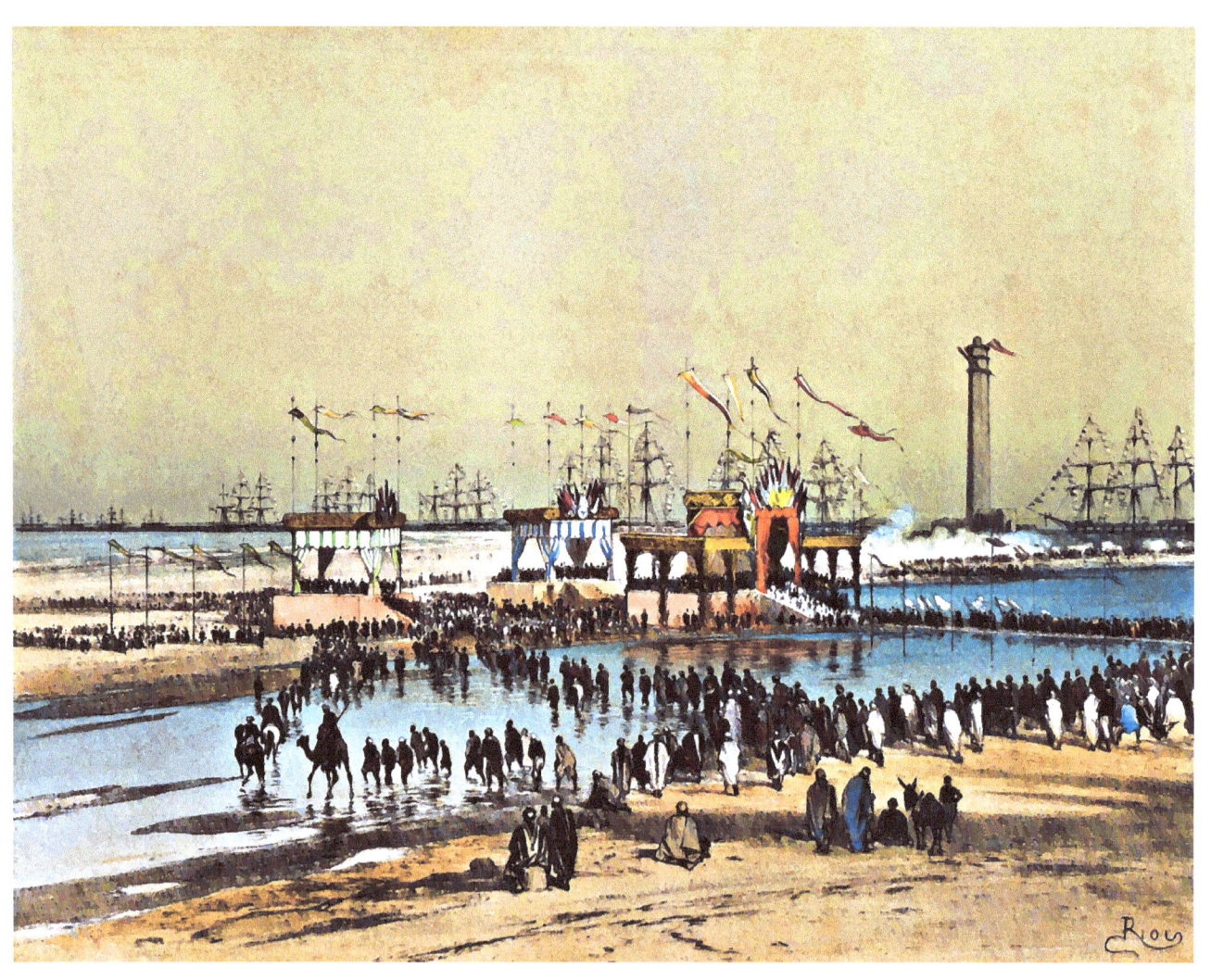

CÉRÉMONIE RELIGIEUSE SUR LA PLAGE DE PORT-SAÏD

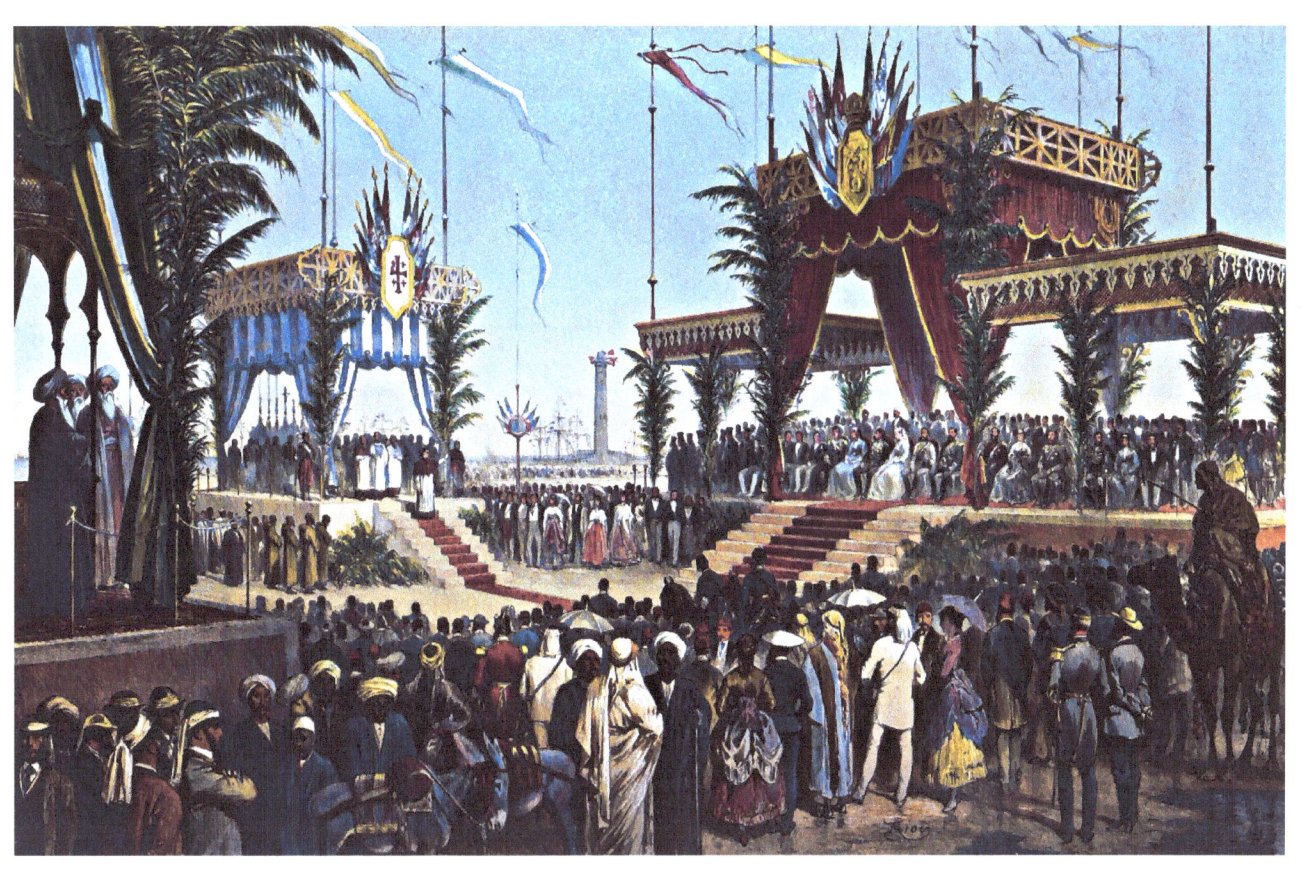

LA TRIBUNE DES SOUVERAINS

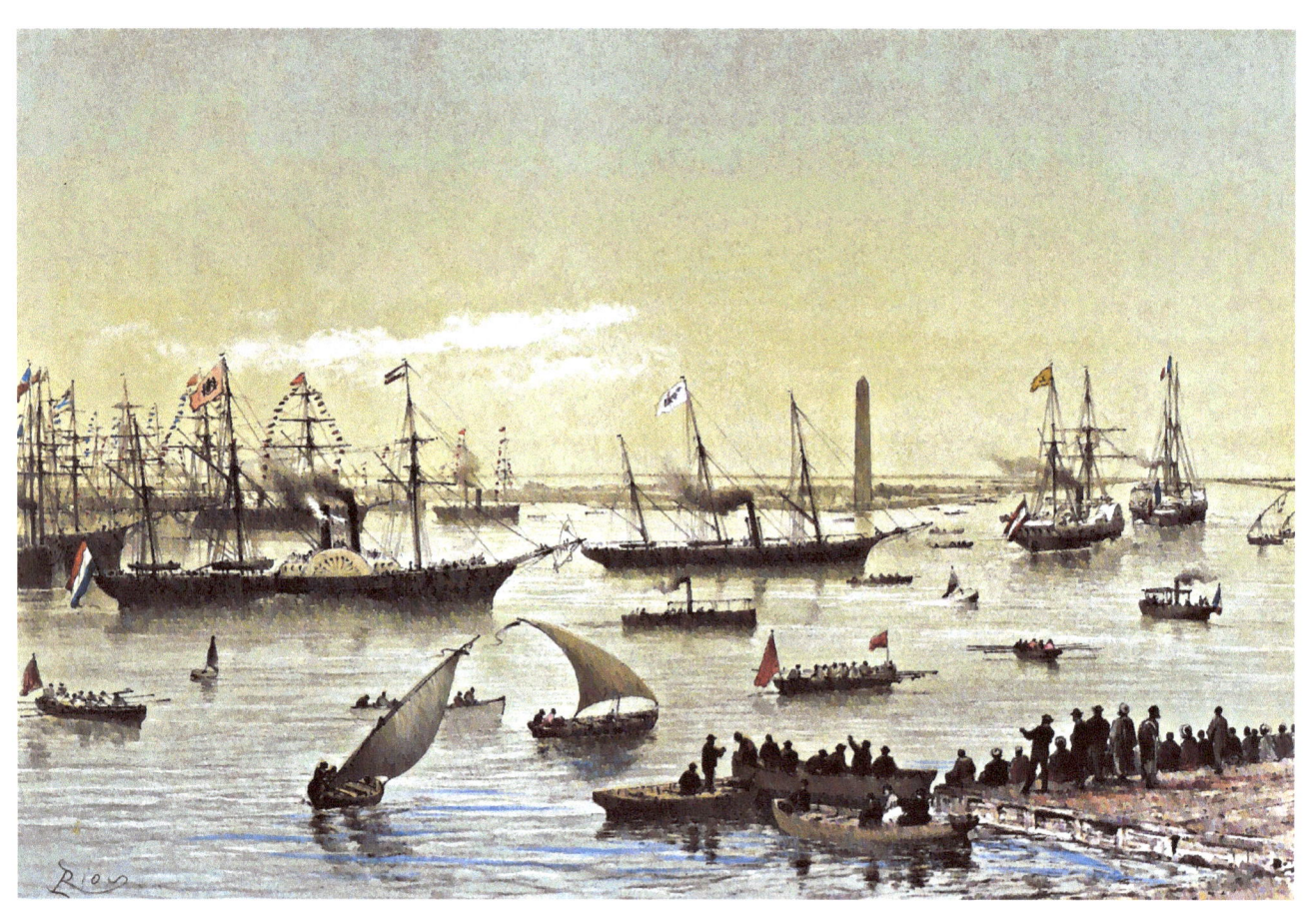

ENTRÉE DES SOUVERAINS DANS LE CANAL DE SUEZ A PORT-SAÏD

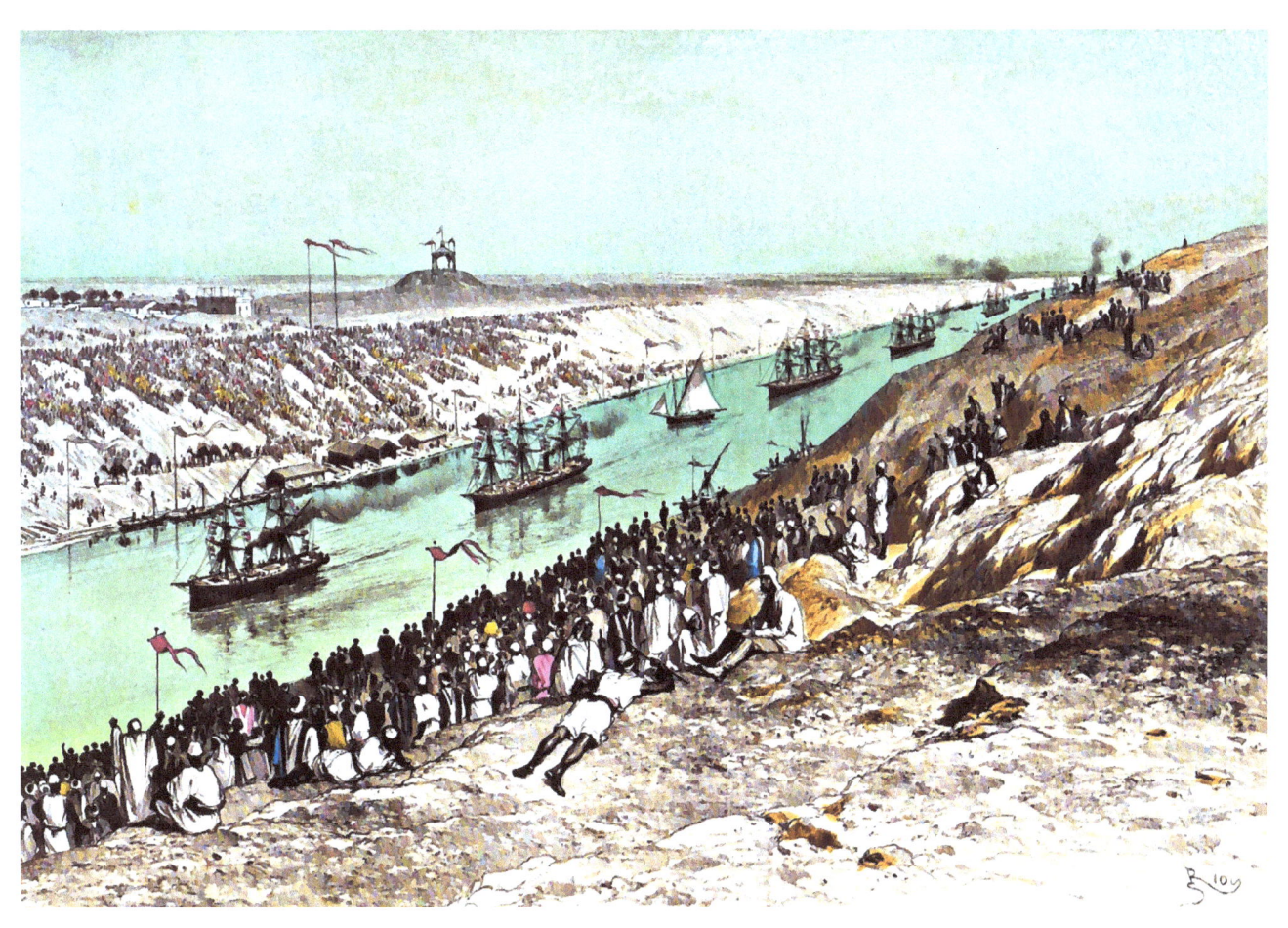

PASSAGE A EL-GUISR

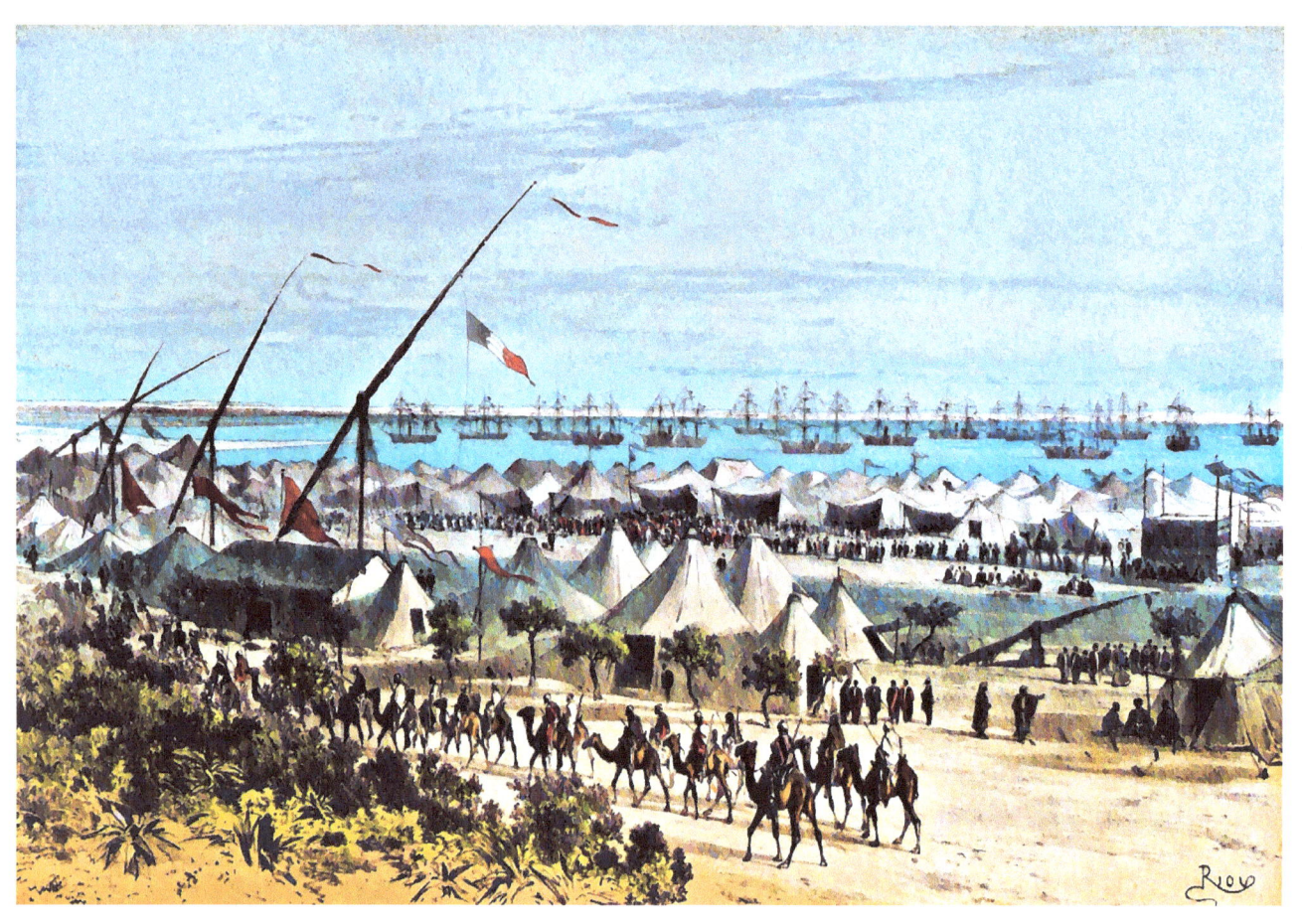

CAMPEMENT A ISMAILIA

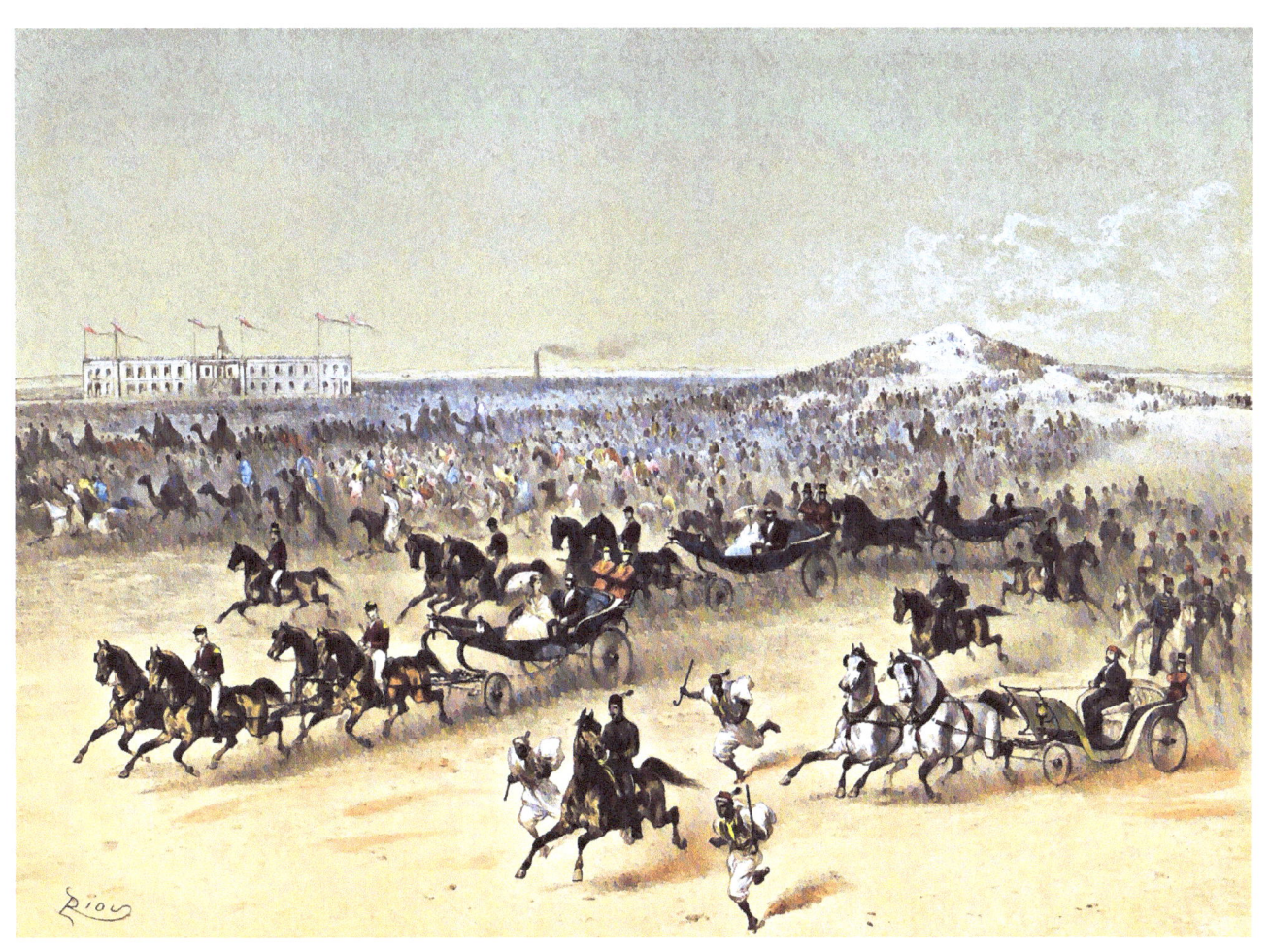

PROMENADE A ISMAILIA

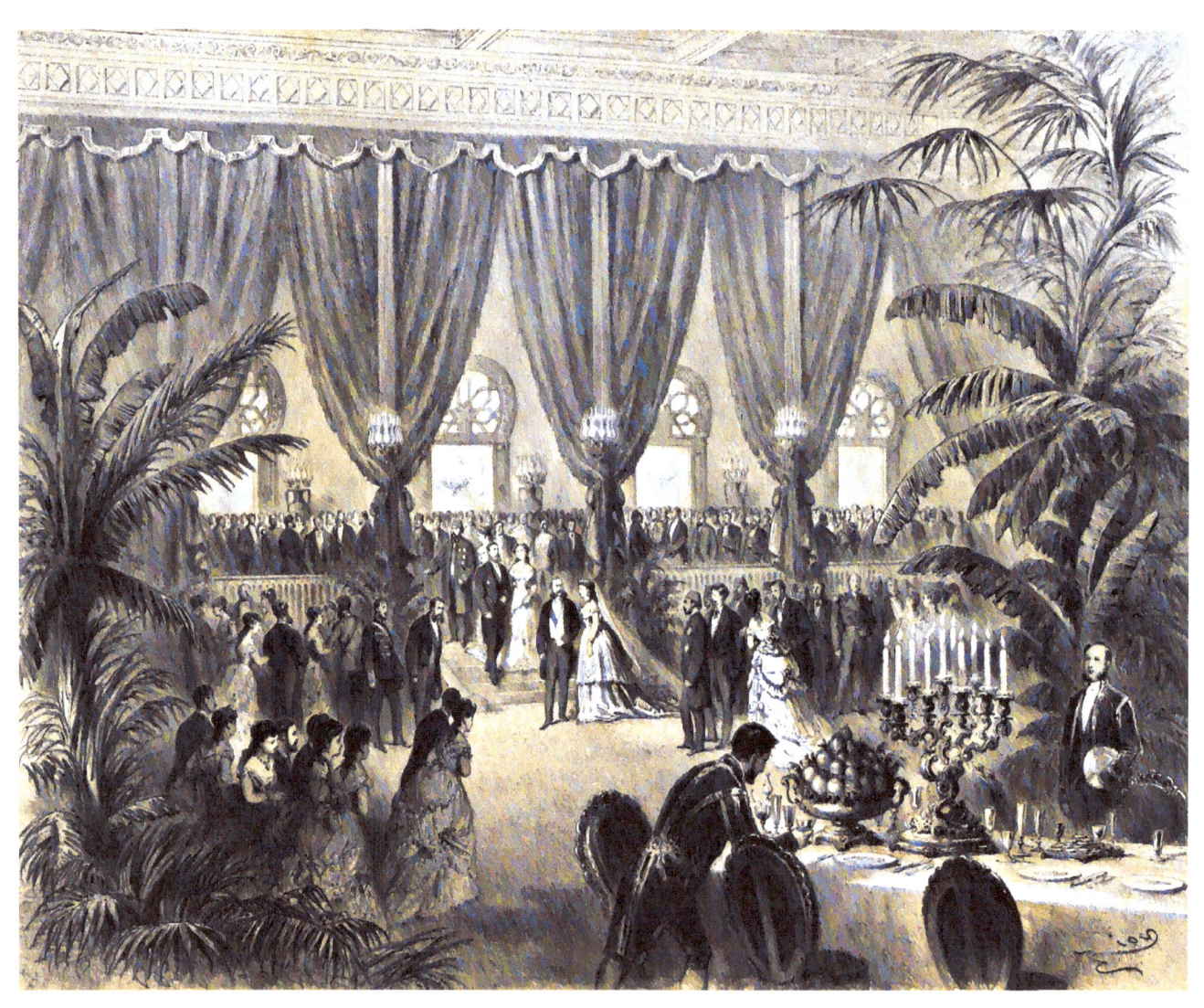

BAL AU PALAIS D'ISMAILIA

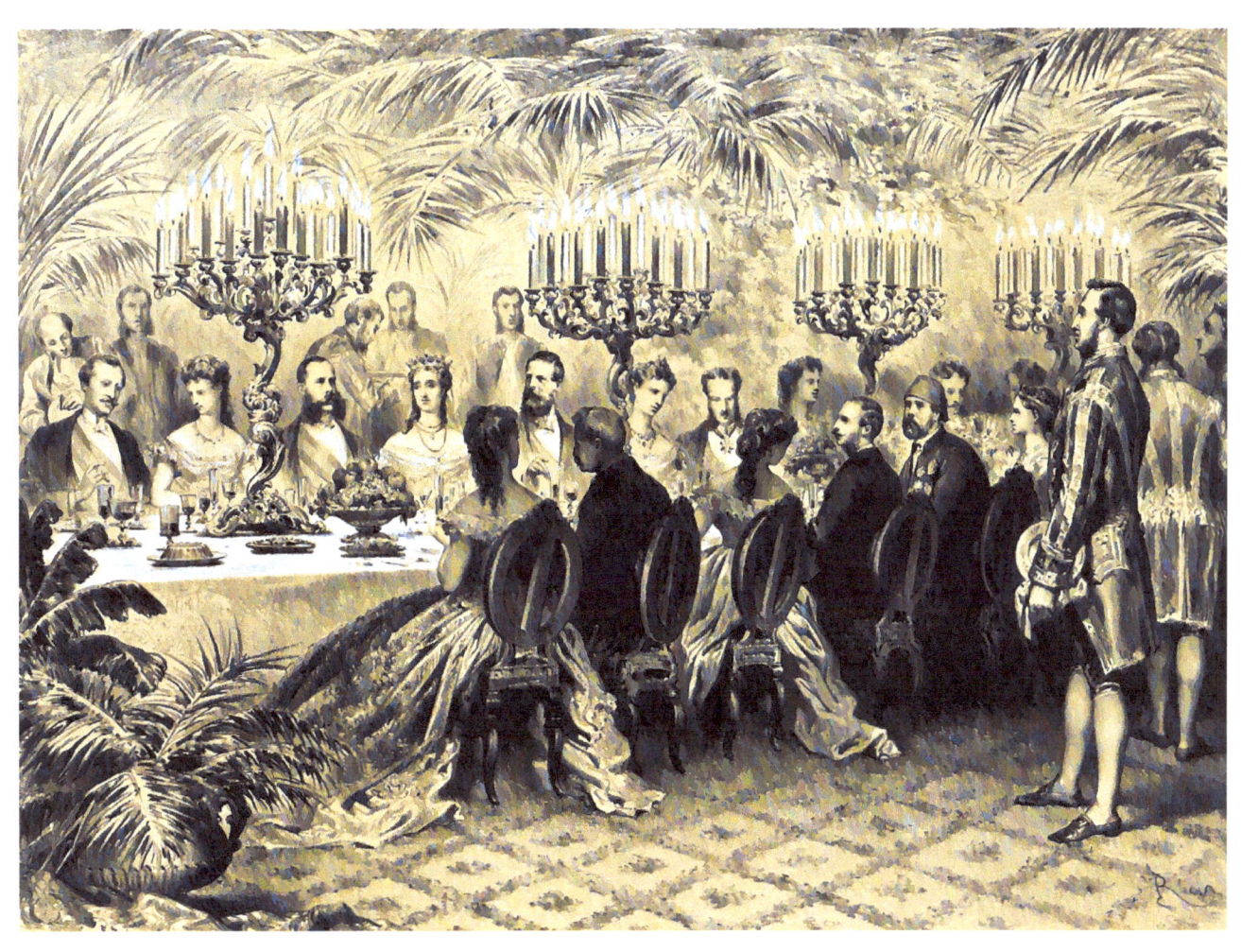

LE SOUPER DES SOUVERAINS A ISMAILIA

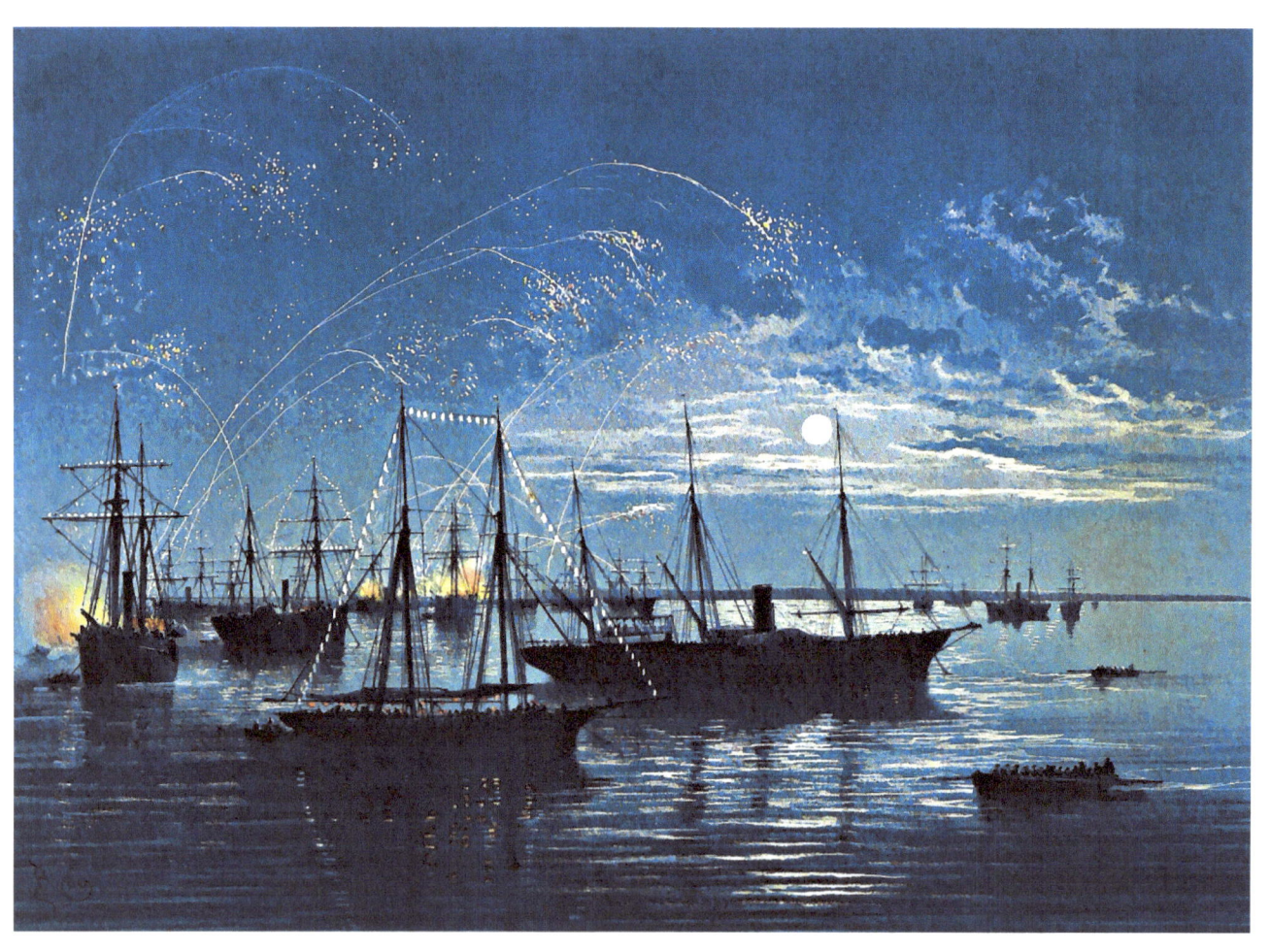

MOUILLAGE DE LA FLOTTILLE AUX LAC AMERS

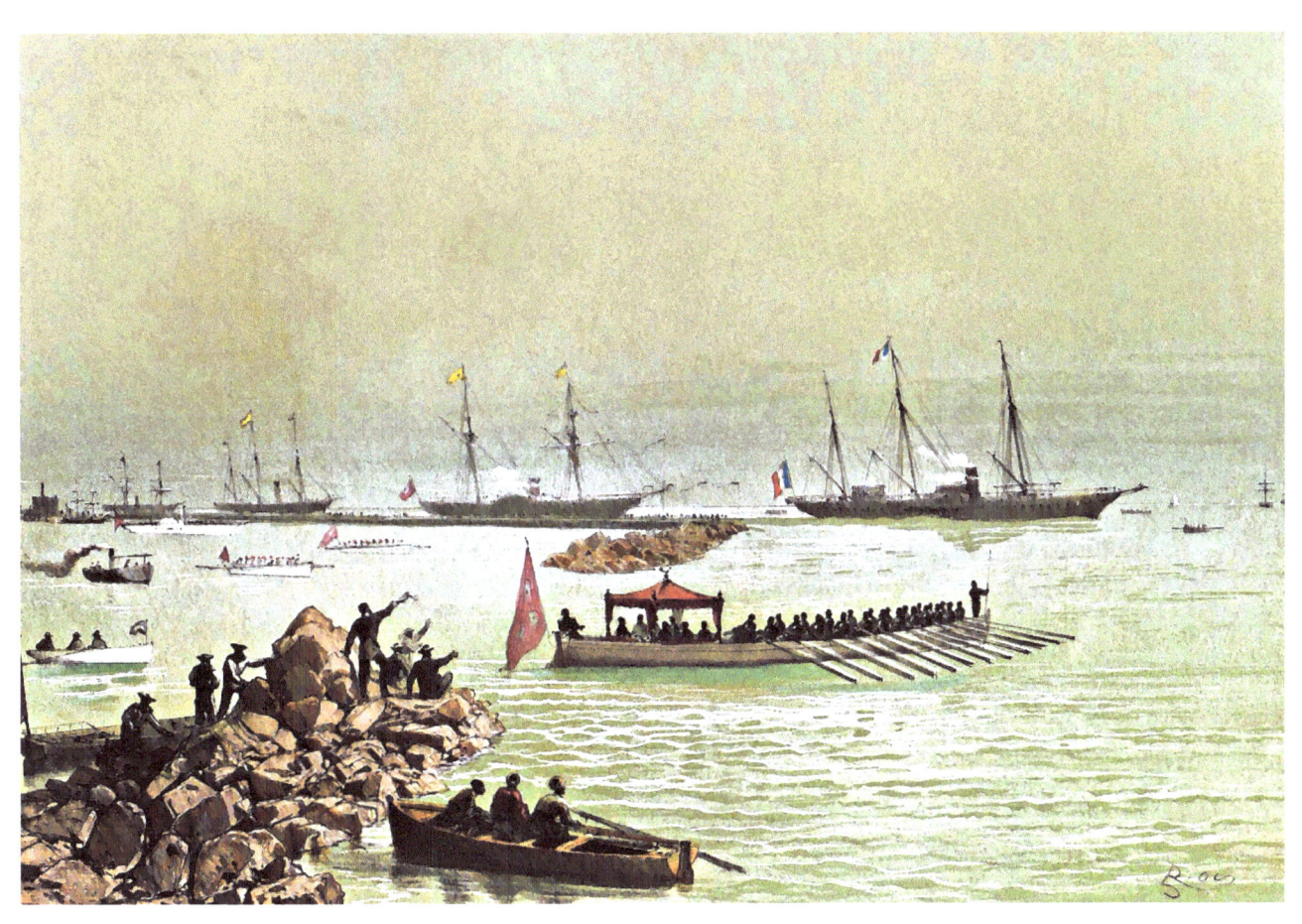

ARRIVÉE DES SOUVERAINS A SUEZ

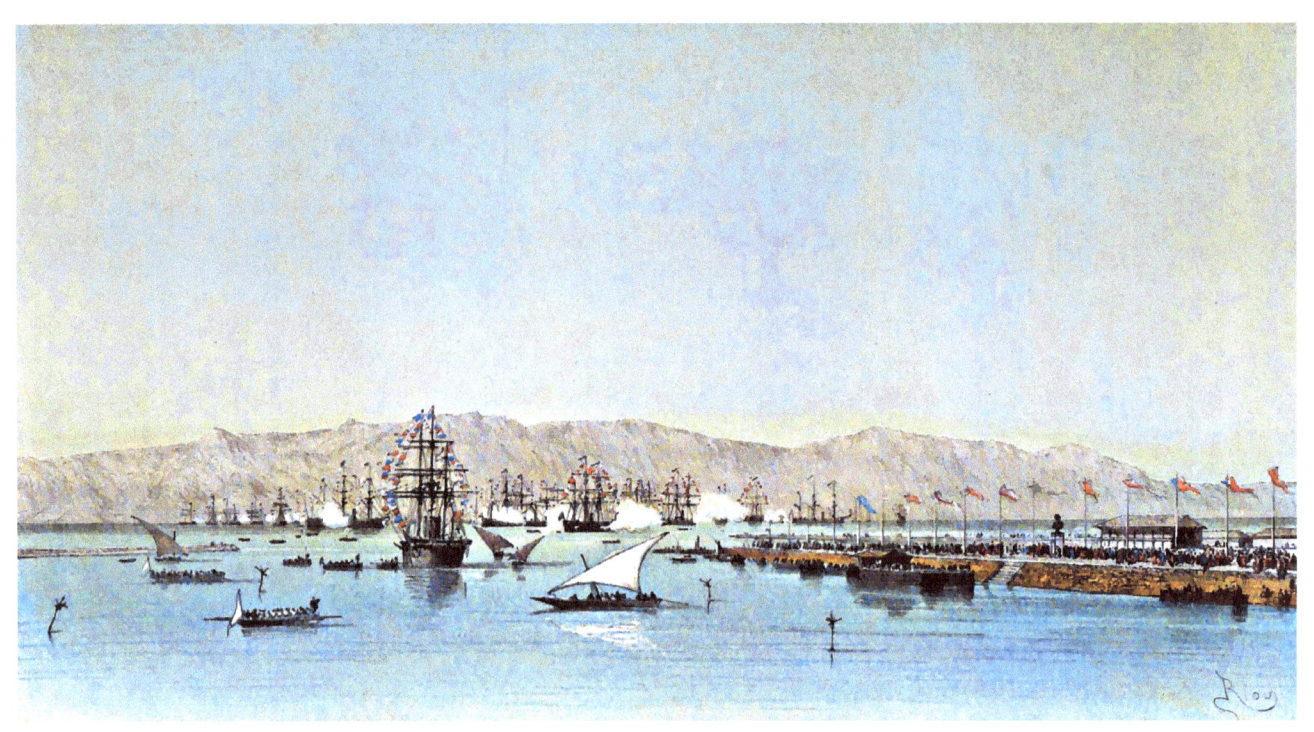

L'ESCADRE EN RADE DE SUEZ

www.ingramcontent.com/pod-product-compliance
Lightning Source LLC
Chambersburg PA
CBHW050833180526
45159CB00004B/1883